Here For It

(the GOOD, the BAD, and the QUESO)

The HOW-TO GUIDE *for* DEEPENING YOUR FRIENDSHIPS *and* DOING LIFE TOGETHER

AMY WEATHERLY + JESS JOHNSTON

BESTSELLING AUTHORS OF
I'LL BE THERE (BUT I'LL BE WEARING SWEATPANTS)

NELSON BOOKS

An Imprint of Thomas Nelson

Here For It (The Good, the Bad, and the Queso)

Copyright © 2024 by Amy Weatherly and Jess Johnston

Published in Nashville, Tennessee, by Nelson Books, an imprint of Thomas Nelson. Nelson Books and Thomas Nelson are registered trademarks of HarperCollins Christian Publishing, Inc.

The authors are represented by Alive Literary Agency, www.aliveliterary.com.

Thomas Nelson titles may be purchased in bulk for educational, business, fundraising, or sales promotional use. For information, please email SpecialMarkets@ThomasNelson.com.

Unless otherwise noted, Scripture quotations are taken from The Passion Translation®. Copyright © 2017 by BroadStreet Publishing® Group, LLC. Used by permission. All rights reserved.

Scripture quotations marked NIV are taken from The Holy Bible, New International Version®, NIV®. Copyright © 1973, 1978, 1984, 2011 by Biblica, Inc.® Used by permission of Zondervan. All rights reserved worldwide. www.Zondervan.com. The "NIV" and "New International Version" are trademarks registered in the United States Patent and Trademark Office by Biblica, Inc.®

Any internet addresses, phone numbers, or company or product information printed in this book are offered as a resource and are not intended in any way to be or to imply an endorsement by Thomas Nelson, nor does Thomas Nelson vouch for the existence, content, or services of these sites, phone numbers, companies, or products beyond the life of this book.

ISBN 978-1-4002-5019-6 (custom)

Library of Congress Cataloging-in-Publication Data

Names: Weatherly, Amy, 1983- author. | Johnston, Jess, 1985- author.
Title: Here for it (the good, the bad, and the queso) : the how-to guide for deepening your friendships and doing life together / Amy Weatherly and Jess Johnston.
Other titles: How-to guide for deepening your friendships and doing life together
Description: Nashville, Tennessee : Nelson Books, [2024] | Summary: "We all long to do life together with people who really "get" us. Amy Weatherly and Jess Johnston, bestselling authors and founders of the wildly popular "Sister, I Am with You" online community, simplify some of the trickier aspects of friendship and give readers practical ways to deepen the friendships they already have"-- Provided by publisher.
Identifiers: LCCN 2023035171 (print) | LCCN 2023035172 (ebook) | ISBN 9781400226832 (trade paperback) | ISBN 9781400226849 (ebook)
Subjects: LCSH: Female friendship--Religious aspects--Christianity.
Classification: LCC BV4647.F7 W3834 2024 (print) | LCC BV4647.F7 (ebook) | DDC 241/.6762--dc23/eng/20231024
LC record available at https://lccn.loc.gov/2023035171
LC ebook record available at https://lccn.loc.gov/2023035172

Printed in the United States of America

23 24 25 26 27 LBC 5 4 3 2 1

To all the ones who have loved our weird selves.

To all the ones who have trusted us with their hearts.

To all the ones who have been there for the

good, the bad, and the queso.

Amy

To Jess: Is it weird to dedicate this book to the actual author? Probably. Do I care? I do not, because nobody put up with more of my absolute and utter nonsense during the writing of this book than you. You have been patient, understanding, full of grace, and unbelievably forgiving. You have encouraged me during some rough spots and you have laughed with me when everything was smooth sailing. What a beautiful, beautiful thing we have built. I would not want to do this with anyone else, and I could not have done it alone. Thank you for being my partner and for enthusiastically saying yes to this weird, wild, and beautiful adventure. Here's to forgetting every single password we have ever created and to helping other women find a friendship as life-changing and life-giving as ours.

Jess

Aubree, you are *the* friend and you have taught me so so much about friendship. There would be no books by me and no "Sister, I Am With You" without you. Your intentionality, authenticity, acceptance (of me in every mood and season), and sense of humor have literally changed my life. Thank you for choosing me. Thank you for loving me, my kids, and my family so well. Thank you for being an enneagram six and teaching me that being uncomfortable isn't bad. Thank you for reminding me of the time you found a McDonald's cheeseburger in my purse. I love you.

Amy, I absolutely couldn't imagine taking this journey without you. Thank you for trusting your gut and reaching out all those years ago. You are one in a million, my friend—the real deal, a true treasure. Also, thank you for teaching me about Texas country and lime and salt on chips. If anyone who works for Taylor Swift is reading this, please hire Amy to write some songs. She is an actual lyrical genius, I'm not even kidding. Kthankyoubye.

CONTENTS

CONTENTS

PART 2: RECIPES FOR DEEPENING YOUR FRIENDSHIPS AND DOING LIFE TOGETHER

Serve with Chips, Drink It Through a Straw, Eat It Like Soup—We Won't Judge.

Hey, it's Jess and Amy again. We were absolutely floored by the outpouring of love for our first-ever book, *I'll Be There (But I'll Be Wearing Sweatpants)*. Our hearts and souls were woven into the pages of that book, and your responses left us humbled and—at times—in tears. Thank you for embracing our words and for embracing the journey of friendship. Thank you for not letting the words stop within those pages and for creating a movement that we could never have created on our own.

Friendship is so dear to our hearts, and we know it is to yours too. We're honored to write and share about the art of doing life together, about loving each other well, and about stepping out of our own small comfort zones and investing in others.

Because of you we see the cultural landscape changing. We see women everywhere talking about the importance of friendship. We see new voices rising up to empower and equip us in our friendship journeys. Most importantly we see that friendship is being prioritized like never before. We are here for it.

But we still have a ways to go. We're not finished, so we're asking you to join us on another journey. This time we're taking it even deeper and further into the complexities of what makes friendship so beautiful, hard, and worthwhile. Grab your muck boots, because this one is going to take you deeper into the trenches than we've ever been. In this book we're going to expose the rawness of our own hearts, our own losses, our own confusion, our own pain, and ultimately our own redemption. We're still works in progress and we don't have all the answers, but we do know that every step is worth it. We do know that we can do this, and we have to do it together as a community of women.

We don't get to see each other as often as we'd like. Our last time was when we traveled to Nashville for a few nights to shoot this cover. We went to meet our editor, Brigitta, for the first time in real life, and let me tell you—she is wonderful. It's one thing to meet on Zoom, and it's another to slide into a booth and have your very first Nashville hot chicken sandwich topped with some kind of heaven sauce. (If we figure out that recipe we'll share it with you.) It's important that you know that yes, this book is written by us, but there is so much work that goes on behind the scenes by women like Brigitta—who are just as passionate about friendship as we are—and this book couldn't happen without them.

The dream for this book was born in a red booth with sticky fingers and full hearts as we discussed what we wanted to bring you in *Here For It (The Good, the Bad, and the Queso)*. We knew we'd only scratched the surface with *I'll Be There (But I'll Be Wearing Sweatpants)*, and we knew there needed to be a deeper dive, a fuller picture.

We knew we needed a "Now what?" to answer the inevitable

question, "How do I take this from friendship to true sisterhood?" We knew we needed to have a real talk about how we show up for the good, the bad, and obviously the queso. Are you ready? Get a few copies of this for your friends so you can take this journey in real time and talk through all of it. Grab your sweats (obviously). We wear sweat suits like it's our actual job (it is our job, right?).

Make queso. We'll probably eat any kind of queso, but all queso is not created equal, okay? We are known to choose a restaurant based on the quality of their queso, and if I'm honest, I'm still thinking about some I had in Nashville when we went to shoot the cover of this book. That was so good. Gah, we should go back there for no other reason than those nachos. Freakin' nachos of my dreams.

We've combined both of our favorite recipes, and if you get nothing else from this book, make sure you get this:

The Queso That Needs to Get in Your Belly. Right Now.

Ingredients
1 pound (16 ounces) white American cheese, cubed or shredded
1/2 cup milk or half-and-half
1 tablespoon butter
1 can Rotel tomatoes (10 ounce)
Chips for dipping (somewhat optional)
Seasonings (optional):
    2 teaspoons cumin
    2 teaspoons garlic powder
    1 pinch of cayenne pepper

Directions

1. Heat cheese, milk or half-and-half, and butter in a medium sauce-pan on low. Don't get distracted—stir that deliciousness frequently like it matters (because it does). Rome wasn't built in a day, okay? This queso takes some focus and attention, but it will be worth it.
2. Once the cheese mixture is fully melted and combined, add your Rotel and seasonings. You can also add more milk or half-and-half if the queso is getting too thick.
3. Serve with chips, drink it through a straw, eat it like soup—we won't judge.

Notes on the Ingredients

Cheese: Go to the deli to get your cheese. Yes, Velveeta gets the job done, and there's no shame in the Velveeta game. (Once it was on sale for ninety-nine cents at my local grocery outlet, and I—Jess—bought like three pounds, so if Velveeta is your fav, be blessed. We support you.) But we're talking about *the best* queso, and the best queso cheese is found in the deli. Get yourself a pound of white American cheese, or if you're real hungry (or are gathering with friends), get a couple pounds. It will go fast, trust us.

Important note here (we wouldn't steer you wrong): You *cannot* use regular cheddar, okay? It's just going to be like a goopy, stringy, icky mess, and we don't want you to be traumatized, so just trust us.

Rotel: When I told my Southern friends that I didn't know what Rotel was, there were audible gasps and now I get why. Rotel is canned, diced tomatoes and green chiles, and it is magic. There are several kinds—you can get mild, original, hot (yes, please), or chipotle. I recommend the original to start, and definitely try chipotle if you like a smokey flavor. I alternate the two.

Milk or half-and-half: A lot of people use milk in queso, but some people use half-and-half. (I am some people. I mean, why be stingy with the fat?! Half-and-half has never not made something better than it was before.)

Butter: Because butter is awesome. Butter doesn't care who you are; it treats you right. Butter loves you back.

Optional seasonings: I love my queso just how it is, but occasionally I add cumin, garlic powder, and a pinch of cayenne. This is your masterpiece; stir, taste, add, and do whatever the universe wills you to do.

Amy's favorite chips: I like Julio's (mmmmm, the salt), On the Border, pork rinds, or whatever you put in my face, honestly. If it's there, I'll eat it.

Jess's favorite chips: I'm here for Juanita's, and I also am a big fan of the thick, fresh-made chips in the deli. You're already there for the cheese, might as well.

Now find a cozy corner of your couch with your softest blanket and fuzzy socks, make sure you have a plate of chips and queso (don't be shy—you're going to have to keep getting up if you don't load up—trust us), and let's dig in.

Let's dig into the good, the bad, and finally . . . the queso.

Love you all, mean it.

Let's go.

CHAPTER 1

BUT IT WASN'T SUPPOSED
TO BE THIS WAY

Repeat after me: My current situation is not my
final destination.
                                                    —Unknown

It's . . . I dunno. Two in the morning? Three? It's early. Too early.
The sun is still tucked beneath the horizon, and even though
I'm snuggled nicely under my comforter, sleep will not find me.
I flip from my right side over to my left. I adjust my pillow. I flip
it over to find the cold side. There isn't a cold side. Everything
is miserable. I flip to my back, open my eyes, snarl at my husband next to me (sleeping peacefully), and return to staring at the
ceiling.

My stomach is sick and my mind won't stop racing. It's almost
like the ticker tape on the bottom of a TV news story. My thoughts
are spiraling. They're all over the place like toddlers on a sugar
high, and I can't seem to get a good hold on any of them. Except
the thought that maybe I'm not good enough. That one seems to
be stuck. I play it over and over in my mind. The hurt feelings,
the harsh words, the miscommunication. I regret things I said. I

regret things I didn't say. I regret things she did and didn't say. I regret so much.

I grit my teeth and tears well up in my eyes. "How? How did we get here and why?" I demand. Not really to anyone—maybe to the darkness.

I tap out a text and delete it. I think I know there are no words that can fix this, but I want there to be a fix so badly. I'm a fixer. I will dwell, obsess, and anguish until there is some kind of resolution. I want to travel back in time. I want to do better. I want to see the red flags and not let myself ignore every single one of them. I want to get it right this time, because at the moment, things are not right.

I sit up and put both feet on the floor and feel around for the slippers I got for Mother's Day. I grab the old, stretched-out scrunchie on my nightstand and flip my hair into some kind of messy knot. I try to get up for a glass of water, but my body feels too heavy to move, so I lie back down and pull the blanket over my head.

The friendship is over. Being optimistic is one thing. Being stupid is another. I loved her. I still do, I guess, but it's all sinking in that I may never see or talk to her again. I don't know if we'll have another interaction, and I don't know whether I'm relieved or heartbroken. Gah . . . how weird is it going to be if we do run into each other? How hard is it going to be to act like she's just some stranger when we have held each other through rough patches and laughed our way through endless girls' nights? How hard is it going to be to pretend-smile and small-talk?

"Ohhh, we're good. The kids are great. How are y'all? It's been so long."

Yeah, it's been so long. We were in each other's lives and now we're not, and that sucks. The memories stay but the friendship leaves, and this was not the plan. At all.

Hey again. It's Jess and Amy. We wrote the above story together because we've both been there, and we bet you have too. Tossing and turning over friendship heartbreaks is awful, and it's also normal. In this book we have more bricks to add as we build our friendships. But we have to warn you, some of these pieces come from the wreckage of our own hearts. From the moments we've stared at the mirror with tears running down our faces while muttering under our breath, "But why?"

This wasn't how the story was supposed to go. We created a beautiful friendship. We built a solid foundation. We dug into the research. We did the things. And now that beautiful love letter is ripped into a million pieces and scattered everywhere.

When we wrote our first book, a lot of our friendships were in solid places. We felt more belonging than we ever had. We'd hit the jackpot and finally found our stride. Friendship was still weird and imperfect and awkward, but we were doing it well. We'd been through the pain, the brokenness, and the loneliness. We'd planted the seeds and were in a season of enjoying the sweet, sweet fruits of our labor. Yes!

And then life happened (it tends to do that), and things we thought were solid got shaken up a bit. We found out some roots didn't go as deep as we thought, and some went even deeper than we knew. If that's where you're at right now, please know you're not alone, and please know it's normal. Sometimes our lives feel like they're getting stripped down to the two-by-fours and the trusses, but it's not all bad (even when it feels like it).

We'll be honest: It's easier to write from the mountaintops. It's easier to write when you're filled up to overflowing. The words just gush out. Writing when you're in the valley is more vulnerable. It's a little more raw, and we think it has a little more grit to it. But it's us, so relax. It's still kind of funny, because humor is our second-favorite language (after chips and queso).

One day recently I (Jess) sat in my therapist's office and lamented that friendships had been so hard and broken and messy lately. I'm getting better at therapy, I think. I used to accidentally over-explain the unimportant details of my life and then crack jokes, and if she laughed, I felt like I was winning at therapy. *Wow, what a good session. She thinks I'm hilarious.* I'm told this is not what therapy is for. I mean, I guess it's a little much to pay to practice comedy. I've also been working on getting to the point of my explanations. As I walk up the long steps to her office, I think, *What is it I'm wrestling with? What do I need to get to the bottom of today?*

And then I plop in her chair, grab the throw pillow, put it in my lap, situate my coffee for easy access, silence my phone (except the kids), and say, "Well, I'm feeling real insecure about this book I'm supposed to write."

"Tell me more about that," she says.

"Well, as you know, some of my friendships have been a real dumpster fire lately. Like, I'm over here smelling the fumes, covered in ash, thinking, *I can't wait to share these beautiful stories with my readers.* What am I going to write? 'Hi guys, friendship is hard. I have no answers, my life is a crapshoot, the end'?"

I get a small laugh from this, and that already makes me feel better about this therapy session. (I said I'm working on it, okay?) "I'm not feeling like much of an expert over here. Like, what am I going to write? A bunch of sad stories of struggle? No one wants to read that." I finish with my eyebrows up and my hands open. Fix me, therapist, please.

"You think what you're going through is unrelatable?" she asks.

Geez, she gets me again with all this wisdom. "Well, I guess not . . ."

"I think many, many women go through friendship losses just like this."

I consider the fact that if anyone knows what many women struggle with, it's probably a therapist. She sees her words sink in and she goes for the gold. "What if this is exactly the book that's needed?" she asks me. "What if this is exactly the book you're meant to write and that women have been waiting for?"

Struggle is confusing sometimes. I think it makes us feel isolated and alone, but I'm not really sure why because every single one of us struggles. The human struggle is one of the most powerful forces that brings us together, if we let it. I'm reminding us again at this moment that we're in it together. We can build beautiful things. We can build beautiful lives, beautiful friendships, beautiful careers, and beautiful families. There's magic in that. We're empowered to build and create.

But sometimes the most beautiful things slip through our fingers. It doesn't mean they didn't matter. It doesn't mean they weren't important. Sometimes it's the opposite.

We've all lost things we built and treasured. Maybe it was a career you put your very heart and soul into. You saw a future there, and when it ended, you didn't know who you were anymore. Maybe it was a marriage. You built something and now you're watching it come down piece by piece. Maybe it's an estranged family member or someone you love that you lost to addiction. Or you had to move from the town where you spent time building deep roots. Or a friendship that you treasured and cherished has crumpled before your eyes. I don't know what it is for you, but sometimes we build extravagant castles only to watch them get washed away by the incoming tide.

We can't avoid the pain in life (God knows I've tried). We can do our best to build things and give ourselves the best chance of success, but life does not offer guarantees like that. We hit rough patches. We weather storms. We suffer loss.

Life really does bring us seasons. Seasons of blooming like spring. Everything is sprouting and growing and there's so much hope and life. Seasons like summer, when we bask in the glory of the sun and when laughter and joy come easily. Seasons like fall, when the colors are beautiful and we're harvesting from seeds we've loved and nurtured into fullness. And winter. Yep, there's also winter. When everything seems dead or dying, seeds go dormant, and life feels cold and harsh and unfair. When we can't see the fruit of our labor at all, we just have to trust that someday soon the sun will peek out again. The sun's warmth will reach our skin. Someday soon the snow will melt, the ice will thaw, and spring showers will fall, accompanied by the sun to bring life back to the grass and flowers and trees. I can't be sure why it works like that, but it does.

All I know is that spring looks even more beautiful after a long winter.

In this book we're going to talk about it all, and our hope and prayer is that it offers you hope, that you feel us gently taking your hand and saying, "You're not alone." We're here for it. The good, the bad, and the queso.

This is the full story of friendship. This isn't the fairy tale and it isn't the tragedy. It's the full circle, which involves a little bit of each, I suppose. When we love hard, sometimes we lose hard, but love is still the way to go. It's still the cure. It's still the answer.

I (Jess) recently visited the town I grew up in. I went to a spot that was really special to my family. It was in the mountains, and a fire had swept through a couple of years before. I hadn't been back for over a decade, and there was this one tree I hoped was still there. It used to have a tire swing and housed a family of squirrels in the springtime. This tree was an iconic part of my childhood.

As we came up on the site, nearly everything was burned to the ground. Trees were charcoaled and broken; the new grass that had grown around them was already dry and golden in the stark summer heat. We rounded the corner, and there it stood like a beacon of hope. I could see where the fire had kissed its trunk, but it was still strong and regal, unshaken. The long hollow that ran down its trunk and used to house the squirrel family was still there. The branches were full of this year's leaves. A lot was gone, but more remained.

Like the tree, friendships meander through seasons of loss, when things are burned to the ground. We've experienced plenty of loss since we wrote *I'll Be There (But I'll Be Wearing Sweatpants)*, but the friendships that have lasted through the winter months and have made it to see the springtime (and thank goodness my and Amy's friendship is still as strong as ever) stand tall and regal, a beacon of comfort and hope and promise. A beautiful reminder that friendship is worth the work.

The thing is, this quote attributed to Hilary Stanton Zunin is true: "The risk of love is loss and the price of loss is grief. But the pain of grief is only a shadow when compared with the pain of never risking love."

There have been times when we've felt unqualified to write on friendship. I (Amy) never truly knew imposter syndrome until this year, but wham! When it hit me, it hit me hard. Learning who I am again has been a process. Who am I to talk about friendships when I'm in the midst of such a messy fallout? Am I up for the job? Was I ever really up for the job? I've experienced disappointment and I've disappointed, and I wasn't fully prepared for either.

But perfect has never been our style. Preaching has never been our tone, and filtered, fake, and polished has never been our approach. We've never come to you pretending to have it all figured out. There is no line between the real version of us and the book version of us. There is only us. And we prefer to keep it real and raw. Well researched, of course, but still gritty.

And maybe, just maybe, this is exactly what women need to hear. Maybe this is exactly what *you* need to hear. That life is ever changing, and we are ever evolving. We're learning each step of the way. Some steps move us forward and some move us backward, but we all end up where we're supposed to be. This book and these words are exactly what they were always meant to be. Maybe it wasn't in our original plan, but it was in God's original plan.

God created us to love. And to love is to act. And to act is to have relationships, to sit with others, to encourage, to be encouraged, to feed the hungry, to clothe the naked, to serve, to have grace, to celebrate, to mourn, and to get down on our own knees and wash some feet with an abundance of humility.

Do we still believe in friendship? Oh, absolutely. It's not even a question. We believe in it with our whole hearts. So please, pull up a chair. Our table is long and wide and there's plenty of room. Sit with us (hopefully in your sweatpants), and let's talk about friendship: the good, the bad, and all the messy parts in between.

We'll bring the queso because—let's be real—the best conversations always happen when we're sharing stories, secrets, and a never-ending basket of tortilla chips.

We've divided this book into two parts. The first is "Recipes for Working on Yourself and Showing Up," because it always starts with the ball in our own court, self-reflection, and looking inward instead of pointing fingers outward. The second part is "Recipes for Deepening Your Friendships and Doing Life Together," because there's more to say and more to do as we journey forward together.

In our first book it felt right to go back and forth by chapter, but in this one we wanted to write together and you will see us alternating more fluidly, exchanging who is doing the storytelling within chapters or both of us writing together in parts. In the hardest stories we share, details have been changed and identities have been protected. It is never our goal to air dirty laundry; however, life isn't just full of magic, wins, and good stories. It's also full of pain, brokenness, and disappointment. We're here for both. We're here for all of it: the good, the bad, and the queso, and we know you are too.

Love,
Jess & Amy

PART 1

Recipes for Working on Yourself and Showing Up

CHAPTER 2

WHEN THERE'S BEEN A STORM
AND ONLY ONE OR TWO ARE LEFT

A Recipe for Grit

> It's better to have one true friend who wants to
> really do life with you—even when it's messy and
> hard—than a thousand friends who are only there
> when things are fun and good and easy.
> —Jess Johnston

I (Jess) always wanted a sister. I begged my parents for one, and though they listened to my pleas, they never ended up giving me one. They did give me a puppy with horrible gas, though, and I loved her almost like a sister. I should also mention they gave me a brother, and he was (is) the best (but also had bad gas) but wasn't good at dress-up and sometimes cut the heads off my paper dolls.

When I was a teenager, I knew these sisters who were really close. They were each other's biggest fans and closest confidants. One of my favorite things about them was the way they didn't have any filters around each other. They'd call each other on their crap. They'd snap and apologize when they were in a bad mood. They'd laugh like hyenas at their shared sense of humor. They were brutally honest with each other, but they were here for it, and it's one of the things I loved about their relationship.

I wanted friends, but even more than that I wanted a friend who was like a sister. I wanted the safety of knowing we were in it together, come hell or high water. I wanted to choose someone and have them choose me back, even when I made mistakes or snapped because I was in a bad mood.

When I was younger, I was constantly searching for that one friend who was a best friend, a sister. I collected best friends like Lisa Frank notebooks and stickers, but it never worked out the way I pictured it and I couldn't figure out why. But then I read that my personality type is a huge flirt. This was confusing for me and everyone who knows me (particularly Graham, who is married to me) because when it comes to flirting, I am really, really bad. It was the great tragedy of junior high and high school for me. Think Josie Grosie when a cute kid introduces himself as Guy.

"YES, YOU ARE A GUY. QUITE A GUY. OH MY. HEY, THAT RHYMES! YIKES. BIKES!"

Other times I resorted to small acts of violence—like when the boy I liked said I had cute toes and I kicked him in the face. Believe me, Graham did not choose me according to my flirting skills.

But a couple years ago I realized that I have focused all my flirtatious energy on friendships. From the time I was five years old I was trying to collect as many best friends as I could on the playground. Whoever I was with at that moment was my best friend, and I made sure to tell them so. This got awkward when my best friends changed multiple times throughout the day and created some uncomfortable playdates where I found myself in the middle of heated friend-triangles. The truth was, I really did feel like I was best friends with whoever I was with when I was with them. I also longed for the safety I thought I would find in a best-friendship. For some people it's shotgun weddings—for me it was professions of long-term friend-ffection after about one minute of knowing them.

"YOU LIKE CHEESE? I LIKE CHEESE! WOULD YOU LIKE TO BE BEST FRIENDS?"

Even now, watch out if you're near me when I have my first latte of the day. With that euphoric energy coursing through my veins, I'm highly likely to suggest taking a trip with whoever is nearest me. *Hello, new friend, I like your shoes. You know what would be awesome? Trekking in France. We should take those shoes to Europe and trek together.*

I do have a best friend/sister now, and her name is Aubree. What I've learned is that true best friends aren't created in impulsive moments of connection but over time. They're created in the good, the bad, and the queso (see what I did there?).

One night, after the kids had fallen asleep, I was mindlessly browsing Netflix when I got a text from Aubree. You up? But before I could respond, I got a call.

"MY WATER JUST BROKE AND IT'S EVERYWHERE AND CAN YOU COME."

I ran into our bedroom and turned on the lights. My husband lifted his head, squinting and blinking. "Whaaat?" he said, disoriented.

I was in go-mode. "No time to talk," I announced. "The babies are coming, bye!" I didn't even put on shoes. I pulled on a hoodie and ran barefoot to my friend's house. I flew through the door to see her standing calmly with a bag in her hand.

"My water broke and it is everywhere," Aubree said. "I think it's even on the wall." My friend was pregnant with twins, and we'd been anxiously awaiting this day. Her eyes were wide and she started to laugh. "Look right there on the painting. That's amniotic fluid." We both broke into hysterical giggles. "Don't sit on the couch," she said. "It's like I dumped a five-gallon bucket right there."

We cackled while her husband raced around the house, looking for the keys and grabbing his extra clothes. It was like the scene in *Father of the Bride Part II* when George puts on Nina's blouse. We hugged, I took a picture, and they were off. I checked that the older kids were sleeping before I fell into a restless doze on the couch (the one without amniotic fluid). In the middle of the night I woke up to a text on the phone that was still in my hand. The twins were here, and they were beautiful.

Aubree and I started out as friends, but now we are sisters, and we have been for a long time. There is no space we're not willing to go, no hardship we're not willing to walk through. We are always learning more about each other because humans are complicated. Am I a perfect friend? Hardly. Is she? Nope (although in my opinion she's pretty close). But the truth is it's okay because we talk about it, all of it. We sit on the floor folding laundry and hash out our hurts. When we make mistakes, we learn and grow. We do life together. We laugh at each other and with each other. We take care of each other's kids, we love each other's families like our own, and—when the season calls for it—we wash each other's amniotic fluid out of the couch cushions and wipe it off the picture frames. We're in it. Barefoot and in our sweatpants, we're in it for the long haul.

I knew Aubree was my person before she knew I was hers. It was ten years ago, and we were riding in the car together to help with a friend's wedding. We had been mildly bickering over flower arrangements, were both stressed and exhausted, and had apologized for taking it out on each other. "Hey," I said, "I wanted to tell you something."

"What?"

"You're my best friend." I was pulling from my playground energy, but I also just felt like I needed to say it.

She looked uncomfortable.

"You don't need to say it back," I said. "Honestly." And I meant it. I just needed to tell her, and I didn't know why. I also don't know why I didn't feel insecure if she didn't respond, but I just didn't. Somehow I knew in my gut we were in it for the long haul.

"I just feel like I can't choose a 'best friend,'" she said. "I have a lot of close friends." She still looked worried, like she was letting me down.

"I actually don't even care if you have a different best friend than me," I said.

"I don't," she said. "I just can't say that yet."

She remembers that moment as super stressful, and I remember it as slightly awkward but also when I realized I had a best friend (even if she wasn't able to say it back yet). It's one of the things I love about Aubree—she doesn't say things that aren't true—she doesn't flatter or stretch the truth.

Little did I know that though I spoke my truth in that moment, it was only a hint of what was to come. I didn't know that we would go on to build the best friendship I've ever had. I didn't know we would move across the country together with our families. I didn't know the mountaintops and the dark valleys we would cross. I would dare to say that at that moment, sitting in the car on the way to a wedding, I didn't even know what a best friend was yet.

In truth, although that moment was the friend version of a DTR, I don't know if you can really create a best-friendship with just your words. I think words can be a piece of it, but true sisterhood is forged in fire.

The last few years there's been a shaking in our lives. It wasn't isolated to one household or person—it's been nearly universal as we walk out of all varieties of trauma. We've had a global pandemic, lost jobs, lost loved ones, stumbled through a world we've never had to navigate before, and so much more that could never be summarized in a short list. We've had all the secondary effects of deep stress, exacerbated anxiety and depression, fatigue and sickness.

We've walked out of global upheaval, where many of us are looking out on wreckage, thinking, *I thought I knew the life I was building. I thought I knew the direction I was headed, and now it feels like a giant reset and I'm right back at the beginning with nothing to show for years of building.*

The thing is, sometimes you don't know who your sisters are until there's been a shaking. I read somewhere that they have earthquake technology that builds buildings on rollers. When the ground shakes, the building stays still. When you look at the buildings in downtown San Francisco, you can't tell which ones have the right infrastructure to withstand an earthquake until it happens. I don't know if there's another way to know the strength of your friendships either. We don't really know if the right infrastructure is there until a shaking happens. I don't wish difficulty or loss of friendship on anyone, but there's something to be said about standing in the rubble and seeing the one (or ones) still there. That moment changes you, and it changes your friendship forever.

I'm sad that friends have moved away, I'm sad that friendships have drifted apart. I feel the loss in my bones. I think those days will come again, but for now I'm learning to be grateful. Some seasons are about abundance, and some are stripping down to the core and valuing the treasures that remain through fire. In my opinion there's no way to build that kind of grit as friends outside of walking through hard times.

A few months ago Aubree came with me to visit one of my besties (who also happens to be my aunt—I can't explain) for her baby shower. We were so excited—we got on that plane like it was taking us to the front row of Taylor Swift's Eras tour. Leaving behind eight kids (and their laundry) with their dads and carrying only one bag each was thrilling.

The trip started perfectly. We had a wonderful dinner out where we laughed so hard I'm convinced my aunt-bestie Melissa's water almost broke right there in the restaurant, and the rest of us probably peed because we've had babies too. On the way back to our Airbnb, we went ten minutes out of our way to get DQ Blizzards and fries, and then we stayed up late watching *Bachelor in Paradise.*

The next morning is when things took a turn, as things sometimes do. I woke up with the stomach flu from hell, but more likely from my daughter's third-grade class. Whatever little barriers were left in our friendship were definitely lost that day in our tiny Airbnb. Aubree smelled smells and heard sounds that day that she will never unsmell or unhear. If she writes a book some-day, she will probably describe me similarly to how I described my puppy and brother: "Lots of fun, terrible gas."

There are some friends you meet that are just your people. Their friendship is built on rollers, and they can withstand any-thing. All I can say is that whatever storm has come our way, I have looked over and Aubree is still there. That day the storm was puking next to her on the couch into a salad bowl and it was just normal.

When you are in a season of loss and saying goodbye, pay attention to the ones who stay, because they are gold. Somehow in all of it you become not just "sisters" but sisters, and even though I'd rather life always be good and full and wonderful, that isn't where best-friendship is truly born. I used to long for a friendship without filters, a true sisterhood. I've found it, but I found it in the hardest seasons of my life.

We've said it a million times, but it can't be said enough: it's better to have one true friend than a thousand kinda friends.

Let me talk a minute to the one left standing after the storm and not a single one of your friendships has made it. I need you to know that even if you look around and there's no one obviously standing beside you, you're not alone. There are so many of us who have walked through that kind of pain, and we feel for you. My prayer for you today is that someone would be highlighted to you, someone you can invest in—maybe someone you've not ever thought of before. My prayer for you is for a deep and resilient hope. There's never a better day than today to start building deep friendships.

The Good

After the storm we see what remains. There's no way to know the strength of relationships without the storm, though it's often unwelcome and unkind. We wish it didn't have to come, but it does, and out of the ashes we find the gold—if we look for it.

The Bad

There's no sugarcoating loss, and that's not what I came here to do. Losing people sucks. Losing stuff sucks. Looking at parts of our lives in ruins sucks. The disappointment of things not turning out how we imagined is real and it's heartbreaking. We can't ignore that pain and that suffering because it's real.

The Takeaway

Have you weathered a storm this year (or in recent years)? Has there been a shaking?

1. Grab a notebook and a pen and jot down what comes to mind. Let yourself feel the heartbreak as you survey the damage of what was lost. Please know you're not alone as readers across the world are reading this chapter and feeling their pain too.

   Solidarity, friend. I'm so sorry for your losses.

2. Now let's visualize the damage and survey what still stands:

   Who remains? Is there one? Are there two? (Yes, family members count.)

   What can you do to value and treasure these ones who remain? (Remind yourself that one person in your corner is enough—it's actually more than enough. Sometimes I think we get so focused on who we don't have that we forget to treasure who we do.)

3. Send one person a text, and let them know how much they mean to you.

CHAPTER 3

EVEN OLD WOUNDS CAN HEAL

A Recipe for Being Aware, Not Offended

> Growing apart doesn't change the fact that for
> a long time we grew side by side: our roots will
> always be tangled. I'm glad for that.
> —Ally Condie, *Matched*

If you read *I'll Be There (But I'll Be Wearing Sweatpants)*, you know that a few years ago, I (Amy) found out I wasn't invited to something with a group of girls I considered pretty good friends. I was hurt, which is fine. I've always been sensitive toward being left out, and there's nothing wrong with being hurt by that. Hurt is a feeling. We can't always help if we have feelings or not. They're like mosquitos when the first rain of summer hits—they sometimes just show up uninvited, like the pests they are.

However, I realized that I allowed my feelings to become fact. I allowed my hurt to morph into bitterness. In my head I began justifying why I'd been left out, put all the blame on them, and left little-to-no room for grace for them or for myself.

"Well, that one girl is manipulative. I bet she orchestrated the whole thing in an attempt to leave me out."

"They are just a bunch of grown-up mean girls."

"I don't need them. I don't like them. I don't want them. So there."

I took their actions, perceived them as a direct insult rather than simply a crummy thing that happened, and buried it all in my heart until resentment took root and started to grow weeds. This is where I messed up. First, I became offended by things that may have not even been real. I couldn't prove that anyone had meticulously planned this event in an attempt to specifically hurt me. In fact, time would tell that they weren't mean girls. And lastly, I did like them and that's why I was upset by being left out.

My offense got me nowhere. Instead it held me back and hindered me. I pushed those people away. I let this event live rent-free in my head for quite some time. I didn't just drive through Hurtsville on my way to somewhere better—I built a house, ran for mayor, and opened up a cute little ice cream parlor there.

And because I was choosing to harbor this kind of offense deep in my bones, for a while afterward I assumed most people's actions were being done to specifically wound me. In an effort to protect my fragile ego, I pushed them away, too, until I fully believed no one liked me, no one wanted me, and no one would ever include me again.

All those girls did was not invite me. Maybe they thought there were too many people going. Maybe my name just slipped their minds. Maybe I misread the friendship, and they didn't think of me as a good friend after all. Maybe it was intentional. Maybe it was an accident. I'll never know and that's okay. I don't need to know.

What I learned from this proved to be invaluable, however.

My offense was a choice I made. My bitterness was a choice I made. My resentment was a choice I made. And these weren't wise choices. They were choices that only wounded and isolated me further. My goal was to feel less lonely. My fear was that I didn't belong, and by pushing everyone away, I am the one who caused my fear to become a reality.

The only person who was damaged by all of this was me. Those girls weren't upset or dwelling on it. They weren't in a bad place mentally or replaying the scenario over and over and over again. They weren't scarred or building up walls. They were moving on with their lives and relationships while I stayed stuck in the chair I was sitting in when I first learned I'd been left out.

So I vowed not to let my response happen again. I wanted to be a friend to myself first and foremost, so from then on I adopted a "well, at least I know now" approach, which means that I'm aware of their actions. I don't pretend not to notice and I don't paint what happened in a shade of rosy pink glitter when the reality is the skies are gray. But I'm not offended either.

I'm aware I was not included.

I'm aware they didn't show up when I needed them.

I'm aware I don't usually get a response from them.

I'm aware I'm putting far more effort into this friendship than they are, and it doesn't seem to be a two-way street.

I'm aware they aren't choosing me and don't necessarily seem to value my company.

I'm aware they said some bad things about me when I wasn't in the room.

And now that I'm aware and my eyes are opened to it, I can adjust my expectations, my plans, and my actions going forward. And when we make the brave and beautiful choice to adjust our focus, things blossom in places where there was once only a tangled mess of weeds.

Even if this perspective causes momentary pain, it's beneficial in the long haul, and maturity is knowing when to accept a brief hiccup over a lifetime of sickness. It's like letting the doctor give you a shot. It stings for a minute, but if it ultimately has healing power—give it to me. I don't want to live sick anymore. I want power over this pain.

Because now I'm free to water different plants if I need to water different plants. I'm free to expend my energy on something else that's actually ready to grow. I'm free to accept things at face value without reading too much into them or walking in ignorance or creating scenarios in my mind that probably didn't happen (and probably won't happen) while walking around with that hurt strapped to my back. That kind of offense is an accessory that doesn't look or feel very pretty and doesn't do anything to spur us forward in our relationship with God, our relationship with ourselves, or our relationship with others.

We can't let our feelings run the show. We have to take hold of thoughts, or our thoughts will take hold of us. We have to be diligent in making wise choices, or our choices will lead us to places we were never meant to set foot in.

Taking personal offense to slights made against us is easy, but taking the high road is necessary. It's necessary and it's good. Our minds need it. Our hearts need it. It's good for us in our friendships today, in this very moment, and it's good for us in our future friendships as well.

And I think sometimes—not always, but sometimes—if we can be truly honest with ourselves, we will realize that our knee-jerk reaction was to be instantly offended because somewhere down the line, we were previously hurt in the same way, in the same area. An old bruise has been out of sight and out of mind until it got bumped again. The wound is old, but the hurt is fresh. And until we properly treat that wound, it's going to come up and start bleeding everywhere over and over again.

When I started digging and trying to learn why being left out specifically caused me so much anguish, I uncovered some graves from high school. I had honestly believed these were dead and done and dealt with, but I hadn't buried them very deep, and every time new rains came, they made their way back to the surface.

I remember telling my therapist that "people out there have real problems. I have real problems. I don't care that high school was hard. I don't care that I didn't really have friends. I don't care that choosing a place to sit in the cafeteria every day was an absolute nightmare or that the popular girl bullied me and made up rumors about me that everyone believed. I don't care about any of that anymore. I'm not traumatized by it. I'm fine. I've moved on and I don't feel sorry for myself at all. I don't want to talk about it."

And she said, "First of all, it's okay if those things did hurt you. That doesn't make you weak. It doesn't make you ungrateful for the life you have now, and talking about it does not equate to complaining about it. That was a pivotal time in your life. It shaped the way you feel about yourself and the way you felt about other people and relationships. Yes, there are other, perhaps bigger, problems in this world. There is abuse and divorce and loss and all kinds of truly difficult things. I call those capital-T traumas, but it's okay if this was a little-t trauma in your life. I'm not going to make you talk about it, but I think it would be beneficial if you did."

I talked about it. I cried. I cried for sixteen-year-old me who had felt so rejected and so isolated, who didn't understand what she had done to deserve that kind of treatment. I cried for sixteen-year-old me who felt she was destined to sit at tables by herself forever. Who felt unlikeable and unworthy, who tried and tried and tried to be enough for people but still came up short. I cried for sixteen-year-old me who never told anyone besides her mom about the pain she was experiencing and had no idea how beautiful she was, who looked in the mirror and couldn't see anything but flaws and blemishes and a body that didn't look like the cover of the magazines. I cried for sixteen-year-old me who felt like if maybe she was somebody different, things would be different too.

And I cried for thirty-five-year-old me who had shoved all these feelings down, who had refused to acknowledge any of her pain, and who was so terrified of being isolated all over again that she pushed people away before they ever had a chance to even know her.

There was healing in that little office. There was healing in those big tears. And the healing brought about a healthier way to look at things.

I'm not saying I never jumped to being offended again, because of course I did. I'm human, and offense had been my go-to reaction for such a long time. Bad habits can die, but they don't die without putting up a fight.

But like I said, once I figured out that I used offense as a justification to judge, assume the worst, withhold grace, and put up fences, I became pretty decent at setting the weapon down and trading it in for compassion, open-mindedness, and reasonableness. Aware, but not offended.

Being aware doesn't mean you hold it against that person, retaliate, or withhold love. It simply means you are now able to make better, more informed decisions going forward.

I pray this helps you get to this room too. Come inside, my

friend. The door is open. The fire is roaring. The lights are low and . . . do you smell that? Ahhh, it smells like vanilla with a hint of peace. And peaceful people have a way of birthing peaceful friendships.

I'm so sorry if you were left out of that girls' night. The hurt is real, but at least now you know. I know you feel deeply disappointed. I know you feel like the friendship wasn't reciprocated. That's a tough realization to come to, but at least now you know. I wish I could reach through these pages and give you a very real, very long, very close hug. I know those things that were said about you weren't fair, and I know they pierced your heart, but at least now you know. I know you really tried to belong, jumped up and down and begged for them to let you into their circle. I know how deep that ache must have been when they still didn't give you a chance. It brings back some childhood grief, but at least now you know.

Because the thing is, you can't control other people. You've never been able to and never will be able to. You can rewind scenarios. You can toss and turn at night and wonder why they did the things they did. You can question your self-worth and search for their approval, but in the end, their actions belong to them.

You can micromanage. You can make assumptions. You can fill in the gaps with stories you've created in your own brain, but it's not going to help you breathe easier and it's not going to make you a better friend going forward. It's going to make you feel like you're losing your mind, so open up your fists and let it go.

You can't control other people. You can't control whether they like you or invite you. You can't control how they feel about you, how they see you, or what they say about you. You can't control how they read the stories you write, how they see the drawings you create, or how they choose to pick up the things you put down. Trying to control somebody else is like running a race with no finish line. It's going to leave you exhausted and anxious.

Friendship insurance doesn't exist. It's why friendship can be so confusing and so all-consuming. There are never really any guarantees. You may be hurt. Things may go sideways. You may give it your all and still come up short. You may misread the situation and end up really trusting someone who doesn't trust you back. That's the way it goes, and there isn't a way to change it. There's only a way to change your outlook, your perception, and the way you react.

Here's some of my best advice:

Be aware but not offended.

See things but don't take it all to heart.

Get really good at letting other people be themselves and do what they're gonna do.

Get even better at controlling yourself.

You are in charge of you—your words, your behavior, your thoughts, your attitude. Do your best. Treat people well. Love with all you have and then leave the rest out there.

The Good

I've said it once and I'll say it again. Being left out was one of the best things that ever happened to me. Because of it, I've become the kind of friend I wish others had been to me. I wouldn't have the empathy, the understanding, or the same level of compassion if I hadn't walked through my own pain.

The Bad

Sometimes we heal crooked. Sometimes that broken leg just doesn't set right and there's no way to fix it but to break it again and reset it. I know it can be scary, I know you don't want to face the pain, but friend, it will be worth it.

The Takeaway

Where are you at? Are you saying things don't matter that actually do? Do you need to sit down and have a good cry for the girl whose heart was broken?

Stop saying it didn't matter, stop saying you're over it, stop saying you don't care.

Let me tell you what my therapist told me: It's okay if those things did hurt you. That doesn't make you weak. It doesn't make you ungrateful for the life you have now, and talking about it doesn't equate to complaining about it.

Do what you need to do, what you would do for your friend if she was processing the same pain: have compassion.

Maybe it starts with journaling.

Maybe it starts with calling a trusted friend and telling them, "Hey, I need to process some stuff from my childhood. Can we meet? It would help to be able to talk it out."

Maybe it starts with setting up a therapy session.

Friendship wounds are real wounds. Being left out causes real pain. As you step forward through healing and onward and upward as the healthier version of you, this is my mantra, and feel free to make it your own:

Be aware, but not offended. Be aware, but not offended.

Open those fists, and let it go. We've got this.

CHAPTER 4

I SEE YOUR LIPS MOVING, BUT I HAVE NO IDEA WHAT YOU'RE SAYING

A Recipe for Seeing Things Clearly

I would rather walk with a friend in the dark than alone in the light.
—Helen Keller

I (Jess) am going to be straight with you. I'm not one of those moms pulling up to school pickup that makes you think, *Dang it. I wish I was as together as her.*

I'm the one who rolls up in a hoodie and weird messy bun (not the cute kind—the kind that hides rat's nests and random pieces of lint), flings open the door, and a granola bar wrapper and McDonald's cup flutter to the ground like a commentary on the rest of my life. I'm the one who makes you think, *Well, I showered and remembered my purse today. I'm doing alright.*

You're welcome.

My third baby, Oaklee, was all joy and sweetness. She was my first girl and my miracle after two miscarriages. I remember my aunt told me that there's a special connection with rainbow babies, and she was right. I had Oaklee attached to my hip at all times, and I didn't want it any other way. I started giving her pigtails when she had five strands of hair, and I frequented the Target kids' section like it was my part-time job, getting my fix of rompers and headbands. The boys embraced her, too, mostly by feeding her dirt and screaming when she bulldozed their block creations.

Whenever we had people over after bedtime, she would stand in her crib and talk and sing. She didn't want to miss out on a thing and wouldn't go to bed until everyone had gone home for the night. Oaklee had the cutest voice in the world, and if she woke up early in the morning before us, she'd turn on HGTV and watch *Fixer Upper* with Chip and JoJo. She'd make friends on every playground, and she loved to snuggle the kittens that moved in under our porch.

She had many gifts. Coordination was not one of them.

Oaklee tripped over her own feet, fell off chairs, and occasionally ran into doorways. I fondly noted that she got her athleticism and poise from me, since she has a lot of features from my husband's side. I was a little proud of my contribution to the gene pool.

On the day of her kindergarten orientation, I sat next to a woman I knew from town who also has four kids. We chatted while our girls did some activities with their new teachers. Then one of the teachers interrupted us. "Excuse me. Are you Oaklee's mom?"

"Yes," I said, looking up from the paperwork I was filling out.

"Oaklee needs glasses."

"What?"

"Oaklee definitely needs glasses."

"Oh! Okay!" I said overly enthusiastically. "Thank you!"

My friend looked at me, pressing her lips together until the teacher walked away. "Are you learning this right now for the first time?" she asked, her eyes watering, trying to keep it together.

"Yes," I said, failing to control the laughter that was radiating through my whole body. "I just thought she was clumsy," I wheezed, covering my face with my hands. Our shoulders shook as we bent over our paperwork and tried to not look like the "problem moms" of the graduating class of 2029. No one in my family has had glasses, so I had no idea what to look out for, and somehow it had been missed in her well-child checkups.

For the record, it turns out Oaklee is coordinated. She can do cartwheels and doesn't run into trees—she just couldn't see very well. I'm a little disappointed that I didn't pass on my genetic athletic "poise," but hey, I guess you win some and you lose some.

As much as we think that everyone sees the world just like we do, they don't.

I'm convinced that not a single one of us sees 20/20 when it comes to friendship. We all have our own quirks, tastes, and preferences for starters, but we also all have our own brokenness. We have wounds from our life experiences no one can see (maybe not even us) that we take into every one of our relationships.

A few things can obscure our friendship vision. Let's look at each one and what we can do about it.

SOFT SPOTS

All of our hearts have been broken somewhere. We have cracked and sensitive places where we've been let down, betrayed, or abandoned. Each soft spot obscures our vision and affects both how we see the world and our closest relationships in ways we don't even realize.

What can we do?

1. **Be aware.** If we have a big reaction to a small thing, that's a clue. We can do some soul-searching to see if our feelings are all contained in this moment, or if there's something from our past that is lighting those feelings on fire and making them all-consuming.
2. **Seek healing.** If something comes up from the past, we don't have to figure it out all on our own! I've found it helpful to get therapy, as well as to process with my husband, a mentor, or a trusted friend.
3. **Give grace.** You have soft spots, I have soft spots, we all have soft spots. We don't need to identify them all to recognize their existence. Because we're all wounded, every relationship requires a whole lot of grace. Grace for ourselves and grace for others.

One time I gave a blunt opinion to a friend that seemed like no big deal to me. She approached me later to let me know that the way I'd responded had hurt her. I don't have to know *why* my reaction triggered her in order to have grace for her and to learn to communicate in a more sensitive way next time.

We need to honor each other's humanity. We live in a broken world, we are broken people. We should all come with a sticker that says "handle with care." I'm not talking about tiptoeing. I'm talking about being sensitive to our own needs, as well as the needs of others, and not expecting everyone to process things in the same way. We each see the world differently, and that's actually a gift.

COMMUNICATION

I don't know about you, but I've read a text before while assuming the wrong tone and jumped to conclusions. My emotions responded before I had accurate information, and logic and reason went straight out the door. Sometimes what feels true overrides what *is* true. Or maybe you speak a different love language than your friends. (More on this in chapter 13.)

Again, it's important to be aware.

If you're experiencing big feelings in your communication, try tapping the brakes and slowing down. We might speak English or Spanish or French, but that doesn't mean we communicate the same. We've lived our own unique stories and we speak our own slightly different dialects.

Like Ted Lasso says, "Be curious, not judgmental."[1] Rather than making assumptions and bull-rushing with our big feelings, it's important to slow down and be curious. One of the greatest tools I've learned is to approach with curiosity and questions rather than accusations and suspicion. So many big miscommunications have been quickly solved with, "Hey, when you said _____, I heard _____, and that hurt my feelings" and asking questions like, "Is that what you meant?" or "Can we talk about that?"

PREFERENCES

It's normal to assume that everyone likes what we like, hates what we hate, and prefers what we prefer.

I have friends who love picking berries. I would honestly rather take a nap in a museum, and I hate naps and I hate museums (sorry).

My (Jess's) husband and older kids love Avengers movies. I don't know what's wrong with me, but I rarely get into them (except *Iron Man*—I love *Iron Man*).

I really don't like split pea soup (like really really don't like it—*gag me*) but my dad *loves* it.

Whether it's food, music, movies, or activities, we're all so different. We see this in the small things but also in the big things, like how we parent, how we do marriage, what we prioritize, and how we make decisions. I can't tell you how many times I've been privy to conversations that circulate around someone else's preferences when they're not in the room. If you'd allow me, I'd love to grab a mic for this, because I think it's super important: JUST BECAUSE THEY'RE DIFFERENT DOESN'T MAKE THEM WRONG. I think we lose out on so much connection when we try to fit people in a box they were never meant to go into in the first place. We are different. We're supposed to be different. It is so very easy to see the world through our own limited view and criticize people who do things differently.

Just because you think it's weird that a friend chose to homeschool when you do public school doesn't actually make it weird.

Just because you think it's weird that your friend chose to redecorate her whole entire house in a *Pirates of the Caribbean* theme (I don't know, 'kay? I'm just spitballing here) doesn't make it weird.

Just because you think it's weird that your friend never seems to dust her corner cobwebs (okay, it's me, I'm that friend) doesn't make it weird.

It doesn't.

Who gets to decide what's weird anyway? This isn't high school and it's not a reality TV show. We're allowed to be different. We *should* be different.

You can't expect your friends to heal your past. I'm so sorry for the ways people have let you down, hurt your heart, and broken your trust. I'm sorry for every wound that you carry. You didn't deserve that, and it wasn't right.

I wish I could wave a magic wand and make it go away, but I can't. No one can. Our friends can walk with us through the pain, but they can't fill up a vessel that is cracked. They can pour and pour and pour, but we're still going to feel empty.

Healing is an inside job that we have to address with therapy and self-work. If we look to our friendships to fix it, we will be left disappointed. It's like trying to heal a broken leg with a Band-Aid—it just won't work. For example, if you believe you will always be rejected because of rejection you've suffered in the past, that is something that you have to address in your own heart. No friend is ever going to be able to convince you that they won't reject you, no matter how much you want them to be able to (and they want to).

When I was younger I expected my friends to pursue me and I rarely reciprocated. The truth was, I had a wound. I was incredibly insecure about being the initiator. What if they said no? I didn't think I could take it. Or, even worse, what if they said yes, but only because they felt obligated? I believed I had to be invited into friendship, not the other way around. Without realizing it, I put the burden of my own brokenness on my friends. It wasn't fair to expect them to do all the pursuing. It wasn't until I dealt with that and stepped out of my comfort zone that I was able to find healing.

It's so easy to put our soft spots, communication issues, and preferences on our friends (we likely won't even know we're doing it), but it's an unfair expectation and it puts too large of a burden on the relationship. Bottom line is, we can't expect our friends to fill a void that can't be filled by them in the first place. In the same breath, we can't do that for anyone else either. If someone is constantly putting something on you and interpreting your actions through a lens that doesn't feel accurate, consider that they may have some deep woundedness that is impossible for you to address. Don't take it personally. If you can, have a gentle conversation with your friend.

One of the best things I've done for my friendships is to get counseling. I joke that getting coffee with a friend is my favorite because it's caffeine and therapy for under seven dollars, and that's true. Verbally processing what I'm going through in my life, dissecting my feelings, and being open about my real-time struggles is such a gift from my closest friendships, and vice versa.

But they're not (and I'm not) a licensed therapist, pastor, life coach, or Jesus, and it's important to remember the difference. My friends are an absolute treasure, but they have not been professionally trained and they aren't being paid, so pretending they are capable of wading through things like grief, trauma, and deep-rooted patterns really isn't fair to anyone. Your friends can do so many things, but they can't do all the things.

No one will see the world the way we do, and that's okay. But in order to see each other clearly and love each other well, we need to broaden our minds and lose the boxes. The sooner we do that, the more connection we will find. I go back to that Ted Lasso quote all the time. I intentionally remind myself to have a posture of curiosity when I notice something different that I might not understand (yet). Gah, there's just so much beauty in the people around us if we learn to look for it.

The Good

It's a gift to my closest friends and family to work on my stuff cuz . . . I have stuff, and although they're great problem solvers, listeners, and holders of my most sacred secrets, the tools I've gotten in therapy are invaluable.

The Bad

Sometimes it can be exhausting to communicate, especially if your friends are just not picking up what you're laying down and you don't know why, but hang in there. If you feel like you're just missing each other in communication, follow the clues, ask questions, be humble, have grace, and release what isn't yours to carry.

The Takeaway

Is your past brokenness holding you back? Is your impaired vision keeping you from seeing clearly? Realizing you need to do some work is half the battle, so good job. Starting can be intimidating—don't overthink it. Try online counseling or schedule with someone a friend referred you to, and if it's not a good fit, it's okay.

If immediately starting with therapy feels too intimidating, begin by making a list of things that might be obscuring your friendship vision and talking to someone you love about it. Every step you take is a step toward healing.

CHAPTER 5

YOU'VE GOT A VOICE, DON'T FORGET TO USE IT

A Recipe for Speaking Up

Don't let anyone treat you like free salsa,
You're the guac, baby girl, guac.
—Unknown

We don't care if you're an introvert or an extrovert, if you're chatty or quiet, I think every single one of us has experienced feeling doubtful about what we have to offer the world. Have you ever rolled up to a potluck with a bag of chips and suddenly realized everyone else has spent the last two months perusing Pinterest in preparation for this exact moment? The table is lined with Anthropologie platters full of bacon-wrapped cheese, glazed shrimp skewers, and stuffed mushrooms. Where do you place a bag of white cheddar kettle chips in a situation like that? Aww yes, let me just crack this open and squeeze it between the baked brie and burrata. Thank God you didn't go with the

Doritos—at least you brought the bougiest sort of potato chip, if there is such a thing.

I think we've all felt that feeling of inadequacy. Who are we to take up space? We don't even have a ninety-dollar platter to present ourselves on.

Have you ever felt like your feelings don't matter, your stories don't matter, your opinions don't matter, or that your cheesy kettle chips need to be discreetly slipped back into your purse before someone notices? Me too.

I love talking, I do. I love sharing stories and making people laugh, but there have been times when I've doubted that I had anything important to say. I have had whole seasons when I felt constipated with my words, like I couldn't get them out. How do I get my brain to make my mouth move again? I don't remember.

Maybe you struggle with listening, or maybe you struggle with sharing. Maybe you struggle with both (Jess raises hand here). If you've ever felt locked up inside like you have nothing to say, this is for you. If you've ever felt scared of sharing your real, honest thoughts, opinions, fears, and struggles, this is for you. If you're more comfortable being a wallflower than a participant, this is for you. If you're more comfortable keeping your needs and your feelings and your opinions locked up and buried where no one can find them (sometimes not even you), this chapter is for you.

In every friendship you're an equal participant. Read that again. You don't matter 10 percent, or 25 percent less—you matter equally.

You are supposed to take up space. You're a gosh darn person, 'kay? It's never, ever our job to shrink ourselves to make someone else feel important. We can value ourselves and value others at the exact same time.

Are you sharing your thoughts and your needs? If not, let me challenge you to start.

Some people won't know what to do with that, but if they can't make room for you to be wholly you—a human with flaws, feelings, failings, successes, highs, lows, and opinions—they're not your people.

I (Jess) had a friend once that exuded drama like a pig pen exudes dirt. She was a cyclone, and when you were near her, you inevitably got sucked in. I was constantly putting my life on hold to help with this emergency or that emergency, until I eventually realized that many of these crises were either fabricated, exaggerated, or created. She'd become very used to me being at her beck and call. She took up 98 percent of the friendship and I took up 2 percent, and by the time I realized it, it was too late. My role had been established.

Once I woke up to how unhealthy it was, I started to take up space and make my own needs known. I started setting boundaries and stopped catering to her every panicked text and manipulative phone call, and she wasn't there for it. She didn't want to be friends with someone who took up space. That will happen sometimes and it's hard, but the truth was, she wasn't ever my friend. She didn't want a friend—she wanted someone to be codependent with.

It can be comfortable to sit in the role of caregiver, listener, and helper. It doesn't require vulnerability, it doesn't require us to step very far out of our comfort zones. It's good to be in those roles for your friends, but unless you're a paid therapist, it's not your job to play that role all the time.

Being stuck at 2 percent can look like a few things. It looks like being in a friendship . . .

- with someone who is always going through a crisis (real or created). Maybe they always have drama to share, and everything in your life pales in comparison.
- with someone who is really loud, and you'd rather not fight for a place to have your voice heard. You're more comfortable listening anyway.
- that reminds you of how you grew up in a family where you never felt like your voice really mattered, so you naturally believe that is also true in your other relationships.
- where you feel more comfortable taking care of someone than being taken care of.
- where you don't feel your friendships are truly safe for your "real" and messy.
- where every time you get the courage to speak up, someone louder interrupts and takes over the conversation. If that's going to be how it is, you'd rather not talk at all.
- when you just accidentally slip into this role and now you don't know how to break out of it.

Listen, you don't need to become someone you're not (we definitely don't want that). It's normal to have one person in a friendship be more of a talker and the other to be more of a listener. The world needs you exactly as you are. What I'm saying is this: Stop treating yourself like the sideshow when you're the whole dang thing. Stop treating yourself like free salsa when you're the guacamole *and* the queso.

You're not going to bring the same things to the table as someone else (yeah, I'm circling back to the kettle chips again, sorry not sorry). But who you are matters. It matters a whole lot. Don't change who you are—just make sure you're showing up, valuing yourself, and using your voice.

Some people will always treat you like 2 percent. They just will. And if they can't take all of you, they don't get any of you. That's on them.

Some people treat you like 2 percent because that's all you give them. That's on you.

Watch out, because I'm about to encourage the heck out of you. I feel real strongly about this, so I'm not going to mince words. Sit down if you need to, take a deep breath, and read this like it matters because it does.

You matter.

You are a precious gem of a human.

I'm talking to *you*—yes, you. Don't look around you, don't look behind you, I'm talking to *you*.

When you wake up in the morning, the world immediately becomes a better place.

You are a gift to your friends. *A gift*. If you withhold the fullness of that gift, you're not just selling them short, you're selling yourself short too.

Your friends don't need a silent partner in their own journey, they need you in all your mess and all your glory. They need your words, your voice, your *you*. No one, and I mean *no one*, has exactly what you have, the exact personality or the exact story. No one has that way that you have with that thing. You might think what you have is unimportant, that it's not that special, but you're wrong. It is special, and you are special. Even as I sit in this coffee shop writing these words, I want you to know a lump is forming in my throat and tears are welling up in my eyes.

As you read this I want you to know that you matter, but more than that, God wants you to know you matter.

It's important that you believe this. It's important that you value yourself, because no one can do it for you. No one can crack open your shell and let you out on your behalf. You have to do the work yourself. You can do it—I know you can.

Stop treating yourself like free salsa, and don't let anyone else treat you that way either. You're guac, baby girl, guac.

———

I (Jess) have a sister-in-law, Alyssa. She's beautiful, she's hilarious, and she's unbelievably kind. She's one of the most generous people I've ever met as well as being thoughtful and genuine. I've been trying for literally years to outgive her on the holidays, and I've come to terms with the fact that it's not possible. Alyssa also sees the people that others might look past. She's also quiet and not naturally loud or boisterous (unless she gets involved in a practical joke, because she's a huge jokester and it's fantastic).

For a long time not many people got to hear Alyssa's voice. She is quick to shine the spotlight on everyone else, quick to serve, quick to disappear into the background. She was quick to let others take up 90 percent and take the 10 percent for herself.

As a guitarist, songwriter, and worship leader, my brother is used to being in the spotlight. He's a little louder (although not *loud*), a gentle soul, and he and my sister-in-law are wonderful together. They had been married for five years when he was sitting in the living room one day, working on a song. He couldn't get it right and asked her if she'd sing with him.

I'm not exaggerating when I say that her voice is incredible. It is magical—soft and gentle like her, and at the same time strong and powerful, commanding your attention and soothing your soul in ways you didn't know it needed to be soothed. Her voice flows out with perfect tone and melody. It is breathtakingly beautiful in ways I don't know how to describe with words. I have chills writing about it now.

Until that moment, my brother had never heard her sing. He recorded her and sent it to our family. I think we all cried. She had the voice we didn't even know we were missing. She'd held herself at 10 percent, but 100 percent of her is *amazing*.

Alyssa's been singing for years now, on stages at churches and in her own home. She's become more vocal and outgoing, but she hasn't changed who she is or become someone else. She's just started taking up space, space that always belonged to her, and it's absolutely humbling to watch. May we all be like my sister-in-law. May we all notice the places we're keeping ourselves small and holding ourselves back. May we all take the risk of showing up as our whole selves, no matter how terrifying it might be.

The Good

Your voice matters, you matter. You are precious exactly as you are, my friend. Don't hide your light under a bushel—let yourself shine.

The Bad

It's hard work coming out of your shell, especially if you've kept yourself tucked away in its comfort and safety for a considerable amount of time. It's going to take courage, it's going to take strength, it's going to take practice, it's going to take trial and error to allow yourself to be free in ways you've never tried before. Just remember the struggle to break out of your cocoon is part of the beauty of finding your wings.

The Takeaway

Ask yourself these questions:

- Are you holding yourself at 2 percent, or is a friendship holding you there?
- What do you need to do to break out?
- What fears are you facing that are keeping you quiet and small?

Think about this verse: "I thank you, God, for making me so mysteriously complex! Everything you do is marvelously breathtaking" (Psalm 139:14).

You are marvelously breathtaking. Full stop.

CHAPTER 6

I'M SORRY, BUT DID YOU JUST SAY WHAT I THINK YOU SAID?

A Recipe for Listening Well

> With mankind's need to understand and be
> understood, everyone ... must focus on the
> opportunity to raise the bar of listening.
> —Ralph G. Nichols

I (Amy) own two dogs, Lou and Brewster. Lou is an old gal. She's loyal and she's slow and she does this thing where, when you ask her if she wants to go outside, she falls to the ground and plays dead. Yes, like an opossum—but a seventy-pound opossum that literally cannot be moved. She also possesses that old-lady wisdom and she knows good and well we can't move her, so she wins at this game ninety-nine times out of one hundred. But Lou is our favorite.

I know, you're not supposed to have a favorite dog. You're supposed to love all your pets equally, blah blah blah. Sure. And I'm not supposed to have a favorite kid either. Get outta here.[i]

---

[i] I'm kidding. Oh my gosh, please take that as the joke that it is.

Anyway, we really like Lou. Brewster gets fed and gets plenty of attention, but he . . . how do I word this gently? He excites easily and is annoying as all get-out. He jumps and whines and interrupts and literally doesn't care what you have going on—he demands that you listen to him right then and there.

If you've ever listened to me on a podcast and heard a whine and then me thumping around all frazzled, yeah. Brewster gives no cares. If he wants to stand on your stomach while you move from side to side trying to look around him so you can watch the last episode in that murder documentary, he'll do it. It's a lot. Plus, maybe he pees a little too. You just never know with Brewster. Poor guy can't help it. He excites easily (sigh). But guys, I'm totally a Brewster. I don't love this about myself, but it's true. I lack Lou's steady, aloof, take-me-or-leave-me demeanor. I beg to be liked.

And heard.

It's something I've been working on for a long time and something I will probably need to continue mastering until the day I die: sitting back, giving other people the spotlight, and just listening.

Ah, the long-forgotten art of listening and listening well.

For so long I believed (and maybe you believed too) that the goal was to be liked. To impress. To have the funniest jokes and the most engaging opinions. To own the conversation. To sing every song center stage, never handing off the microphone. To make people leave the conversation and go, "Wow. I know so much about her. Isn't she amazing? We simply must invite her along everywhere we go. She will keep us entertained."

But the older I get, the more I realize the key was never to be liked. The key was never to dominate or tell stories that win people over to your side. As though conversations are a game of tug-of-war. Nah. That tactic will be the right key to open some houses, sure, but not every house and not for very long.

The way to open houses, the way to engage in constructive conversations and begin actual relationships, is to give space for everyone to learn about each other. For everyone to have a platform and a spot to say, "This is who I am. This is a little piece of my heart, my mind, and my soul."

That requires connection.

And connection requires listening.

And listening requires shutting up.

And shutting up requires you to come to the realization that a conversation isn't a game, and it's not a way to manipulate, or to demand, or to be like ridiculously-extra-Brewster and think you're the only one in the room with something to say because if someone doesn't give you love or validation right then, you might die. (And not play dead like Lou. Actually die.)

You know what's funny? When I sit back and let the other person take the lead, it takes a tremendous amount of pressure off me. This is good news for people like me who have social anxiety.

I don't have to delight. Instead I can focus on being delighted by the person I'm with. And thank goodness. I have maybe two or three truly interesting stories and after that . . . nothing. I don't know compelling facts. I don't have alluring details to share. I don't even read that much, to be honest, unless we are talking about Taylor Swift, and then I may or may not know the most.

It's truly a beautiful thing to step back, take a seat, hand the mic over to the person in front of me, and learn about who they are. Learn anything about them. Their favorite football team. The best trip they've ever taken. Whether they call them breakfast burritos or breakfast tacos. Literally anything.

This is another human person that God has crafted and formed and molded. A person he loves. And little ol' me has been given the opportunity to engage in conversation with them. How beautiful. How humbling. So when I really try to capture that moment, I typically find three things:

1. **They light up.** People enjoy talking about themselves. It's why so many of us are so eager to do it. It feels good. It's like a little dopamine hit that releases something deep in us. In fact, a study found that talking about ourselves causes the part of our brains associated with rewards and satisfaction to light up, much like it does in regard to money and food.[1] Like . . . I dunno . . . queso.

2. **I like myself better.** I don't wonder if I said the wrong thing. I don't wonder if I was awkward or weird. I'm not nearly as hard on myself and I have no regrets, because it wasn't a show. And since it wasn't a performance, there's no critic waiting to harshly put down my every move. There were two of us, and our names were both on that playbill. We did it together.

3. **I think other people like me better too.** They leave the conversation feeling heard and understood. They leave feeling like someone took an interest in them, and that's nice. We all like to be liked. And when you listen to others, voila! They feel liked, which in turn makes them want to be around you more.

All listening is not created equal. If we can get really good at giving all our attention when someone is sharing, we have learned a phenomenal skill and we're giving an incredible gift. Have you ever shared with someone who is truly invested in what you're saying? Gah, it's precious. I always leave those conversations walking taller, feeling stronger and more grounded. Being understood is one of the greatest keys to belonging, and we have the ability to give that away.

I'll still always tell jokes. And I'll probably always have something to say. There is a piece of me that genuinely comes alive when I entertain and share things. I get excited by conversation and ideas and the passing around of stories. And I don't think it's fair to take that piece of me, squish it into a little box, and discard it.

Every piece of us deserves to shine. But some pieces also need to learn patience, self-control, and when to shine on stage and when to sit in the audience and delight in someone else. Just because these things don't necessarily come naturally to me doesn't give me an excuse to continue in my bad behavior. So here are a few techniques I use to be a better listener.

Tuning out distractions. Yup, this one is really difficult for me. We live in a busy, chaotic, and oftentimes overwhelming world. But if we can learn to silence the noise around us, it is so much easier to become engaged with the person in front of us.

Repeating what you hear. I repeat certain phrases to reinforce that I am hearing what they're saying. If you're not careful, you can make this one weird as all get-out. Don't make your friends feel like they're talking to a mockingbird, but do make them feel like you're really paying attention. Pick a phrase out here and there: "Oh wow! You're from Louisiana. I've never been there, do you like it there? What's it like?"

Pausing to think. I bite my metaphorical tongue and practice the very literal pause. *Is what I'm about to share worth sharing? Will this opinion/statement/story add to the conversation, or will it take away from what they're saying? Am I just waiting for my turn to talk, or am I actually listening to them? Am I interrupting?* Interrupting is what Brewster does when he pees all over the place, and nobody likes that.

Following up. I make some kind of leading statement, then I wait for their reply and ask at least two follow-up questions. For example:

> **Me:** I've never been to this restaurant before, but I love the ambiance.
> **Them:** It's my absolute favorite, I come as often as I can.
> **Me:** Oh, I love that you come here regularly. There is something about a familiar setting. What is your favorite dish on the menu?
> **Them:** The salmon is insane. Sometimes I dream about it at night.
> **Me:** Salmon. Do you have any good recipes for making it at home? I'm always looking for something yummy to feed my family.

I tell my kids that a conversation is like playing a game of catch. Someone throws something your way. You hold it for a second and then find a way to toss it back to the other person. And just like catch, nobody wants to play with a ball hog very long.

Being curious. A great tool for asking good questions is curiosity. Imagine you're hanging out with one of your personal heroes. What would you do (besides panic and freeze, because that would probably be my go-to at first)? You are fascinated with them, so you'd want to know everything. I mean, don't make them feel like they're under investigation, but do let your curiosity take the lead.

Hey Taylor Swift, when did you first know you wanted to be a singer?

Hey astronaut, what was it like setting foot on the moon?

Hey politician, what's it like to be in the public eye? Is it stressful?

Hey musician/actress/author/humanitarian, what makes you come alive?

Me: What do you do for work?
Them: I'm a third-grade teacher.
Me: Oh, that's awesome! I have so much respect for teachers. What brought you to teaching?

They share an important life story about their journey to working in education.

Me: Wow, that's so cool—thank you for sharing that. What are your favorite things about teaching, and what is most challenging?

They get to share on a deeper level about the good, the bad, and the queso (see what I did there?).

Finding connection points. I look for ways to empathize with others' experiences without taking over the conversation. I find the points that link us. Maybe they teach third graders, I have a third grader. I'm pretty familiar with both what is awesome and what is challenging about that age. These are things we can connect on, and these connections are what make life beautiful. The more linking points I can find with a person, the more likely a friendship will develop.

Choosing common interests. You don't have to bring up topics you have no interest in. You're growing, but you're not superhuman. If you couldn't care less about working out, you don't have to ask tons of questions about it. If it's something that matters to them, then yes, it's good to pay attention. It's a special skill to care about the things the people you love care about. But you're going to have a really hard time paying attention if you stay on that topic too long.

If you notice they have a garden and you love gardening, ask about that. If you realize they've spent time in New York City and you've been dreaming of visiting there, ask questions about that.

Finding value. I walk into the conversation with the mindset of, "I'm going to find the gold in this person." Let's be honest, some people's gold is sitting right on the surface. Some people's gold has to be mined a little bit. Anyone can find value in the obvious. I want to be like Jesus and find the value in the less-than-shiny exteriors. For this moment my only two goals are these: (1) Be present and (2) make sure that when they walk away from this exchange, they feel better about themselves, better about the world, or more understood than they did before. It's not about me being interesting. It's about me being interested *in them.*

Noticing passions. Get good at noticing when a particular topic lights someone up. People love to talk about things that set their souls on fire, and they hate talking about stuff that doesn't interest them. If you ask a specific question and you see them brighten, stay steady on that path.

One of the gifts of being a good listener, and digging deeper than the surface, is that we might find friends we wouldn't have otherwise. There are plenty of quieter people in the world who are chock-full of gold and who get easily passed over because people don't take the time to pay attention. Be a noticer. Be a listener. Be curious. Some people are naturally good at this. One of my kids says they prefer listening over talking (and they are good at it), but don't worry if it doesn't come naturally to you. Just like anything in friendship, if you weren't born with it, you can learn it. No one is trying to change who you are, but we can all grow to become the kind of friend we long to have.

The Good

Learning to listen is a skill we can use in every aspect of life. It takes work to form new habits, but we are capable. Take the pressure off yourself to entertain and put a whole lot of that energy into being fascinated by the people in your life.

The Bad

It might feel awkward and uncomfortable at first. You might worry you're being boring or underwhelming. You might have to get used to not being the one on the stage, but the reward of truly getting to know people will be worth it (so worth it!).

The Takeaway

Next time you're meeting up with a friend, practice listening and asking good questions. If you're worried you'll get stuck, jot down some questions you have ahead of time. I love asking people about two things:

1. **Travel.** Where they've traveled, if they like to travel, if they have any dreams or plans of going somewhere specific, etc.
2. **Learning.** What they've been learning lately is bound to lead to some great convo. There are no rules except to be interested.

Everyone has stories, and it's our job to excavate for them. Everyone has dreams and desires, and it's our job to create space to share them. People are wonderfully full of gold—we just have to stop and look for it.

CHAPTER 7

I WOULD RATHER EAT SOGGY CHEETOS THAN ADMIT I'M WRONG

A Recipe for Humility

> To make mistakes or be wrong is human. To admit
> those mistakes shows you have the ability to
> learn, and are growing wiser.
> —Donald L. Hicks, *Look into the Stillness*

Okay, I (Amy) want to die a little just thinking about this story. Like, fall out of my chair, no pulse, no breath *dead*, but here goes. I was at a little neighborhood gathering one night. We had just moved there a week or two before, so while I was friendly with most of the women present, I wasn't actually friends with them, ya know? We were not in the sweatpants phase of our relationship. We were still in the I-want-to-impress-you phase, so I was wearing hard pants or a dress or something. Full makeup. Hair fixed. All of that. I was standing in the kitchen over a charcuterie board, trying to be clever and pretending to be at ease, when in reality my social anxiety was making me want to scream.

Someone mentioned this trendy restaurant in town, and

without pause or thought I blurted out, "Eh, I do not like that place. I just don't get it." There was a girl in the background shaking her head and doing that little shut-up motion with her hand to her neck, but I was not picking up what she was putting down, so I kept going. "I went there last week and the food was not good and it was so expensive for this teeny tiny plate. I'd rather have mozzarella sticks at Sonic than ever eat there again."

First of all, nobody asked for my rude opinion. Second of all, the woman who owned the restaurant was standing right next to me. Like right next to me. There was 0 percent chance she hadn't heard every ugly word I'd said. Third of all, I have never choked on my own foot like I did that night. It tasted terrible . . . like the food at her overpriced restaurant. (Kidding.)

Along with my foot and some cheese and crackers, I ate a lot of crow that night. And some the following day.

There was no way around an apology. There was nothing to do except to accept responsibility, admit my mistake, and let it all crash over me like a wave of intense humility.

Because she's a saint, the owner of the restaurant did forgive me, and because she is one of the coolest people on the planet, we still enjoy each other's company. But that's honestly beside the point. I screwed up, and I needed to tell her so. No excuses, no blame-sharing—just the honest truth. I was a jerk. I messed up and I would never make that same mistake again.

Culturally we are in this dark place where admitting you were wrong or that you made a mistake is the worst thing in the world. But it's not. It's really not. We need to allow room and space for ourselves to err from time to time, and for our friends to err as well.

Our job isn't to defend every decision we make and every word we say, but it is to keep our side of the street clean and to sweep away the thoughtless words we say and the careless mistakes we make.

Of course you were wrong. You're a person. You're not perfect and you're not all-knowing. Maybe (likely) you didn't know when you said that thing, it was going to be taken so differently than you meant it. You did your best. And you got it wrong. Or maybe you didn't do your best, and honestly, I'm not making excuses for it, but that happens too. We're tired and we're spread thin. Sometimes we haven't napped in a while, and we're going to act in ways that aren't necessarily indicative of who we are on the inside.

I think when we mess up, it's important to ask ourselves one question: Is this a pattern? In other words, Am I continually hurting others in this same manner, or is this out of the norm for me?

Either way, the issue needs to be addressed and apologized for, but patterns deserve special attention.

It's weird to say, but in my (Jess's) friendships when I look back at moments of conflict, when handled well, they became moments of great connection. Looking someone in the eyes and saying, "You're right, I messed up, and I'm sorry" is an act of radical connection. You're saying, "I choose to lay my own ego aside, my own defense. I'm hearing you, and I'm making it right, because our relationship matters more than my pride. I care enough to get it right."

Let's not forget that when someone lets us know they're hurt by us, it's often an act of extreme vulnerability. It's hard to say, "You hurt my feelings." We need to make sure we're a safe place for that to happen.

I've both gotten this right and missed it in friendship. I've been on both sides of the coin. None of us are perfect, but we can all work to get better at being wrong.

I always joke that I have no idea what my butt looks like

because I never see it. If I do see it in a picture, I'm always slightly surprised, like, *Does that thing belong to me?* It's bigger than I expected, just kinda hiding back there. Also, on the same note, I rarely shave the backs of my thighs because if I can't see it, it doesn't exist, right? I constantly get stuff in my teeth and my husband tells me, "Your filters are full." There are things we don't see, on our bodies and in our actions. Even if you're not a klutz like me (it's true and I embrace it), I promise there are things you don't know about yourself.

Our culture is obsessed with being right, and it's causing us to miss out on one of the most important gifts of relationships: *having someone see the things in your life that you cannot see.*

We find our peace and self-assurance in believing that we aren't wrong, that it's the other person who is to blame. We find resolve in defending our own case in our heads—and to everyone else who will listen. We want to believe that we are the victim of each and every conflict each and every time.

I've gotta tell you, this mindset is not a great quality (culturally or individually), and it keeps us stunted in our friendships and in our personal growth. Without acknowledging our faults, we run in the same circles, continue in the same destructive patterns, and end up stumbling over the same hole over and over again.

Defensiveness is easy. Self-reflection is hard but necessary. And the reality is, friendship costs us our pride. It's important to have healthy relationships, but there is no way you're never the one in the wrong. There's no way you're never the villain, so if you find yourself always mentally protecting yourself from fault, maybe it's time to ask why.

Listen, it's challenging to open up to someone you trust and to be met by a wall. I know what it feels like to be unheard because someone's ego is right smack-dab in the way of their ears. I know what it feels like to try emotionally communicating with someone who cannot or will not receive it. I know what it feels like to offer a warm apology and to be met by coldness in return. It's hard. You think Alaska is cold in the winter? Nah. Try the heart of someone who isn't emotionally healthy enough to have a heart-to-heart conversation.

I also know what it feels like to be so obsessed with my own self-protection that I'm defensive, unapproachable, and unwilling to move from my self-built throne of stubborn arrogance. When I get like this, my ego may win the battle, but I lose in friendship every time.

Let me tell you something: no friend wants to have to lawyer up to approach you about something you did that hurt their feelings. That's entering the boxing ring when you should be laying your gloves aside, taking their hands, and hearing their heart. If they're someone who loves you, the truth is they are *for* you. Even if they say it wrong, even if they communicate imperfectly, you have to cling to the knowledge that they are *for you*. If you don't really believe they love you and are for you, why are you even friends?

For me, all I know is I want to choose humility in my relationships (however painful and awful that may be). I don't always do it well, in fact sometimes I don't even see my pride for what it is, but Rick Warren is right: "Pride builds walls between people; humility builds bridges."[1] Sometimes you build the bridge and someone else builds a wall.

A friendship can only continue to grow and deepen if you both build bridges.

The truth is, when we build bridges we also leave ourselves open to feedback.

Our closest friends have the ability to see things in our life that we don't see. That's why it's called a *blind spot*. If we don't trust them to speak into our life, who do we trust? To me, friendship is a safety net. Even though it's hard to hear that I have things in my life I need to work on, I'm thankful I don't have to be on my own.

The thing is, when we build bridges, when we get close (real close), we see each other's real (and it's not always pretty). It can be intimidating to let people close enough to see our fine lines, wrinkles, and that pesky chin hair that grows overnight, but the truth is that it can be a gift.

One of my friends and I used to run errands together all the time when our kids were little. I often ended up driving since, at the time, I had four kids and she had one. After probably ten drives together, she looked at me like she needed to say something (or was possibly constipated).

"What?" I asked.

"Are you going to drive any faster?"

"Huh? Am I driving slow?"

"You are driving the actual speed of a grandma tortoise, and every time you start talking, you drive even slower, if that is *even* possible."

We burst out laughing, "Sooorrry," I said. "I'm not great at multitasking."

"No. No you aren't. Also, your windshield wipers have been on for twenty minutes and it hasn't rained since Tuesday." Tears were forming in the corners of her eyes as she snorted. "You do this all the time, and I've been really wanting to tell you."

To this day I (mostly) remember to turn off my windshield wipers because of that friend, and to this day if we go somewhere together, I ask if she wants to drive because I have a lot of things to tell her and that way we can get there in under an hour.

Y'all. It's okay to have blind spots. And it's also okay to be wrong. It really, really is. People who are never wrong are not very enjoyable people. It's no fun. On behalf of all the people who love you, please stop it. *Relax* and take a deep breath—we're all learning. Let your guard down. It can be embarrassing to have someone hold up a mirror and say, "Hey, did you know you do this thing that you do?" or "Hey, when you do this it makes me feel _____."

So what? Buck up. Be wrong. You can do it. I promise.

You survived the time you clogged the toilet at a youth retreat and everyone found out. You survived the time you got onstage during your school play and said someone else's line before freezing like a human mannequin for an uncomfortable amount of time. You even survived not making it to the bathroom that one time in the aisle at Hobby Lobby (you know the time).

YOU CAN SURVIVE THIS, TOO, and you will be better for it.

Listen, friend, you will never (and I mean *never*) be capable of great and deep friendship if you don't learn to clean up your own messes and mistakes. Here are two tips on cultivating humility in your everyday life:

First, be approachable. It's hard, scary, but important work to be a safe place for your friends to bring something up. If defensiveness rises up in your chest, take a deep breath. Work to hear what they're saying with both your ears and your heart. If they truly love you and are for you, it's probably hard for them to bring this up. Maybe they didn't communicate it perfectly, maybe they could have said it better, but try and remember they're doing something scary for them and have grace.

Second, get good at apologizing. Picture that you walked into your friend's house and you picked up their favorite platter. It slipped out of your hands and crashed to the ground, breaking in a million pieces. What do you do?

1. **You own it.** "Oh my gosh, I'm so, so, sorry! I know how much that platter meant to you and I broke it. I was moving too quickly, I should have been more cautious."
2. **You don't** tell them they should have put the platter in a

safer place. You don't blow it off like it doesn't matter (if it matters to them, it should matter to you).

3. **You clean it up.** You get the broom and the dust pan and you get to work. If it's repairable, you spend tedious hours gluing it back together. If it's replaceable, you work to find the exact same one you broke, and if you can't find that, you get something better. Friend, you just got upgraded from Target to Anthropologie.

4. **You don't** leave the mess on their kitchen floor. You don't not do your best to make it right.

Apologies are hard to give. Mistakes are painful to admit. And tough conversations are awkward to approach, but I've never had a friendship that burned to the ground because someone was brave enough to own their mistakes. I have had plenty that were lost because of silence, avoidance, and a need to be right. In the end, you can have your pride or you can have the friendship, but you can't have both. So choose to walk in humility.

The Good

Humility gives us ample opportunity for growth. We don't become who we're supposed to be without relationships, without people occasionally calling us on our crap. I knew someone who has been married no less than ten times. When things got hard, they moved on. When their spouse asked them to change, they left. No judgment to them, but that person's flaws and issues became bigger and bigger until they passed away.

We don't have to change, and we don't have to grow, but if we want to become the best version of ourselves, that is the only path forward. My father-in-law hates to prune his trees because they always look so sad afterward. Cutting them back never looks pretty when it's happening, but he knows it's worth it in the years to come. Those trees produce more fruit than they ever could without the pruning, and they always come back prettier than before.

The Bad

Sometimes we make good on our mess and the other person doesn't. We swallow our pride and listen with ears that listen. We recognize that blind spots are called blind spots for a reason. If a friend brings up something that we don't think is accurate, we consider it and we ask other friends if they see it too. We do the work. But that leaves no guarantees that our friends will do their work too. We talk about it in the next chapter, but friendship really only works if we both keep our side of the street clean. Just remember, you are only responsible for yourself. And I don't know about you, but I want to be the kind of person who is approachable. I want to be the kind of person who chooses growth.

The Takeaway

Ask yourself these questions and answer them honestly:

1. How do you respond when someone approaches you about something you did that hurt their feelings?
2. Are you quick to defend yourself or quick to make amends?
3. When you make a mistake (and you know it), what do you do to make it right? Do you clean up your mess?

Now (if you're really brave) ask your friends or family the same questions (about yourself). Ask them if you are approachable. Ask them if they feel heard and validated when they bring something up.

Remember this is hard work, and we're all just learning and growing together.

CHAPTER 8

SOMETIMES PEOPLE SUCK

A Recipe for Grace

> When people show you who they are, believe them.
> —Maya Angelou

W e're about to say something that absolutely every single one of you will agree with (yes, that's a big ol' statement). Sometimes people suck. They just do. We can believe the absolute best in people and we can love them. We can make lots and lots of excuses for them, but at the end of the day it's still true: sometimes people suck. *Drops mic, bows, leaves stage.*

Just take a moment with me to think about the last time a person sucked in your life.

That lady who rolled down her window and flipped you off (WHEN YOU ACTUALLY HAD THE RIGHT OF WAY, MA'AM)? That was sucky behavior.

That friend who betrayed you in the fifth grade and told everyone your secret crush and you felt like you couldn't face a single human again for months? She might be the bee's knees now, but she sure as heck sucked back then.

The ex-boyfriend? You know the one. The one who left a big ol' mark on you with their suckiness.

That woman who gave you very aggressive, unsolicited advice when you were barely keeping it together with that tantrumming toddler in the candy aisle? SUCKY BEHAVIOR, LADY.

The friend who broke your heart recently? The one who left a meteor-sized hole when she walked away? Sometimes people suck, man, just call it what it is.

The truth is, we're not trying to have grace for people who don't rub us the wrong way or who never hurt us or disappoint us. We're trying to have grace for people who sometimes don't even deserve it.

I (Jess) grew up in a family that prioritized loving people exactly as they were. It didn't matter if they thought differently, acted differently, or believed differently—they were our friends and we loved them as equals (because that's what they were—equals). My dad was a pastor in our small town, but he believed his job was to serve people and never to judge them or change them.

I don't ever remember a time I heard my parents talk down about or bad-mouth anyone. I know that's an extreme statement, but it's true. Because of their example, grace has always been a big deal to me. In particular, not judging people who live differently than I do. It has always confused me when people feel it necessary to weigh in on others' choices. Like, why?

I truly believe we would find a significantly deeper level of connection if we all put judgment in the backseat and let grace ride up front. We might even find we have much more in common with the people around us than we ever realized. We might also find amazing friendships in unexpected places.

We have to stop expecting people to be like us. We have to stop being the *Mean Girls* of friend hunting. (You aren't required to wear pink on Wednesdays in this friendship, but if you want to, that's cool too. Also, if you know us, you know sweatpants are *always* allowed.) People are weird and quirky and unique, and it's a gift if we let it be.

I'm not very detailed or observant. I would probably not notice a cobweb if it grew across my entire living room and a spider rolled up my cat into one of those bundles to eat later. I break things, drop things, and lose things all the time. I'm currently buying my daughter more hoop earrings because I borrowed hers and have no idea where I put them. I'm very aware that I drive some people crazy, and it's okay, I get it. I'm not everyone's cup of tea.

One time my husband was describing my quirks to my brother-in-law, who asked how Graham dealt with it. (My husband is detailed, observant, and doesn't break, drop, or lose things.) He said, "I just decided I was going to think it's cute, so I'm not annoyed about it."

That man, he's a national treasure. Let's be like Graham.

We don't have to be friends with everyone, and if they really, really annoy you, it's probably not a good idea to be close friends. We have different tastes, interests, and priorities. We have different personalities, beliefs, and life experiences. Some of us like climbing huge mountain peaks, while others get all their needs met strolling the aisles of Target. There are people who dedicate years of their life to study and become doctors, and on the exact same planet there are people who make a living creating YouTube videos pranking people. Some of us love to travel and explore the world, while some of us love nothing more than to stay home, snuggle up, and stay comfortable right in our own living rooms.

I think the world is kind of like an abstract painting. As someone who is not an art connoisseur, when I see abstract paintings, my first thought is, *What is that?* My second thought is, *So you're saying I could paint like a toddler and charge tens of thousands of dollars for it?* But if I take a step back and appreciate it for what it is, abstract art is beautiful. It doesn't make sense, but I don't think it's supposed to.

In an article on understanding abstract art, Thaneeya McArdle writes:

> Abstract art doesn't jump out and declare "THIS is what I'm all about." Instead, abstract art requires you to have an open, inquiring mind. . . . Look at abstract art in the same way that you would listen to a symphony. When you listen to music, you don't try to hold on to the notes—you let them wash over you. Let your eyes wander over the painting the way the notes of a symphony wash over your soul.[1]

What if we looked at the people around us just like that? What if we let the different notes, brushstrokes, and flavors that they represent wash over us rather than trying to understand them or control them?

There's another level of grace, though, and this one is much harder and more complicated.

It is grace up close.

As an adult I've learned that grace at a distance is much easier than grace all up in my face. Having grace for the people I've given access to my heart is much less straightforward or simple. It's messy, it's painful, and what I believe in my head is the "right way" to handle things gets murky.

Grace is a nice idea, but it feels a lot easier to implement when actual people aren't involved. People who hurt us. People who suck. People who betray our hearts. People we trusted who were not ultimately trustable. People who did something awful to someone we care about.

The thing with love and opening up our hearts is that it's always a risk. We don't want it to be, but it is. Every single time. When we open our hearts, we give people direct access to hurt us. They have a line that goes straight to all of our most vulnerable places. Straight to our insecurities. Straight to our past rejections. Straight to our fears.

The truth is, though, that without risk, there will never be deep, meaningful friendships.

Nobody wants the risk, but oh, how we all want the reward. You wouldn't haven't picked up this book if you didn't crave the reward of friendship. I wish I could untangle the two, but they will always be tied together. Sometimes on the end of that rope will be a friendship that carried you through, held you up, and stayed with you until the very end, and sometimes on the end of that rope will be a friendship that fizzled out.

When one of those closest to me hurts me, I might put on a brave face. I might try to say the right words and pretend like I believe the things coming out of my mouth, but it's a lot harder than just talking the talk. It's a straight-up battle to walk in grace when the pain hits deep. I smile. I go through the motions, but the battle waging war in my mind is real. It can become this all-consuming combat that attempts to destroy everything. I don't sleep well. If it's an especially bad situation, I can't eat. The events roll through my brain over and over until it takes over everything else. All the good in the world gets harder to see. All the good in people gets harder to see too.

This is hard for me to admit, but when my heart has been shattered while dealing with close friends or family in the past, I've abandoned all grace and I've said things like this:

> "I know it's wrong, but I think I hate them."
> "I want to want good for them, but right now I just want them to get what's coming to them."
> "I want to tell everyone that likes them the truth about who they are."
> "They are a blankety-blank-blank."

Things get a lot messier when we're hurt. A lot messier and a lot harder. Sometimes it feels impossible to let the person who wronged us off the hook or to release them with forgiveness. I've prayed for grace in moments where all I've felt was white-hot rage. I've learned that I have to be patient with myself to get there. It's more complicated than sticking a Band-Aid on the wound and calling it good.

The truth is, people *do* suck sometimes and it's a disservice to our own hearts to not let that be real. It's not our job to rationalize other people's mistakes or play down our own pain. Grace is a lot easier said than done, especially when we're reeling from an injury to the heart. Just like most things, real grace and real forgiveness can't happen without letting ourselves experience real hurt.

Many years ago I went through a friend breakup that completely blindsided me. I had been all-in on this relationship, and I found out in a very painful way that they didn't feel the same way. This was one of my *people*. Someone I planned on being friends with forever. This was someone I'd invested countless time and energy into. We'd already been through thick and thin, better or worse, so I believed our bond could withstand any storm.

At the end of it all there was no closure, no resolve, and I felt completely misunderstood. How could she not know me better than that? How could she believe, after all we went through, that I was capable of the awfulness she was accusing me of? How could she launch those kinds of arrows at my weakest spots? I was so incredibly hurt that even now I cannot find the words to adequately describe it. A building that took years to construct fell to the ground in a matter of days until all that remained were a few memories and a gargantuan pile of trash.

I was even mad at God. *How* could this be ending?? A relationship I considered so safe was gone overnight. How could God let me go through this? What was the point? Why had I missed the signs and why hadn't I invested elsewhere?

The aftermath of that friendship wasn't pretty—for a long time. And if I'm perfectly honest, from time to time ugly thoughts still creep in. Like I said, I still lose hold of it sometimes, and I have to fight for it all over again. My fight for grace was all uphill and it was messy and broken.

I wanted to judge her.

I wanted to misunderstand her.

I wanted to think the absolute worst of her.

I wanted to stay angry with her.

I wanted to blast her to everyone we knew. I didn't necessarily want to be the victim, but man oh man, did I want her to be the villain. I wanted everyone near and far to be just as mad as I was, as if having company aboard this misery train would somehow comfort me and calm my battered and bruised feelings.

I struggled. I struggled through the pain. I struggled with rage. I struggled to get ahold of my mind. But most of all, I struggled to find *grace*.

It isn't easy (by a long shot), but my parents taught me that grace is worth fighting for—in ourselves and in our friendships. Maybe part of what makes grace so powerful is that it doesn't come naturally. It isn't something that's handed to us and it isn't something that's tied up with a pretty little bow. It's something we work toward—an abstract painting we have to step back and decide to see.

My parents didn't give grace only when it was easy. They showed me what it looked like to extend it when it was hard, like when someone they'd cared deeply about started using drugs again and lost custody of their kids. When someone they'd helped after that person got released from prison went back to prison for committing the same crime. When people they loved started blaming them and resenting them and pushing them away.

Bottom line: grace says everything about us and nothing about the other person.

When I ask myself if I want to be a woman of grace, the answer is yes. But that comes at a cost, because like I said, grace isn't handed to us. We have to choose to pick it up. And I hope we do. I hope we do choose it.

I don't believe a single one of us is going to reach the end of our lives and think, *I wish I would have stayed more offended. I wish I would have stayed more rooted in my bitterness and resentment. I wish I would have been angrier. I wish I would have been less gracious and held more grudges.* No, I don't think so. Grace frees us to go out and experience the life God has laid out for us because yes, sometimes people suck, but our purpose is to never let them suck the life out of us. And if we're honest—if we're really, really honest—I think we can all admit that sometimes we suck too. None of us is getting through without an abundance of grace thrown our way.

The Good

No love given is ever lost. I truly believe that. It's scary to keep opening up our hearts and giving away our love to people who might hurt us. It's super scary. But your love, it still mattered, it still made an impact, it still changed who you are. Carry on, warrior. Loving well is still the way to go.

The Bad

People do suck sometimes. It's just a fact, and those people are going to affect us with their suckiness. They're going to hurt us, they're going to disappoint us, and they're going to betray our trust. Friendship is never going to be as safe or uncomplicated as we wish it would be.

The Takeaway

Vent to your closest people. Tell them the truth of your own thoughts that feel icky.

Write a letter holding absolutely nothing back, and then toss that letter in the fire.

Have it out with God or scream at the universe while you're driving alone.

Go on a run that ends with sobbing on the beach.

I've done every single one of these things.

Dig deeper than just the anger. You might feel like the red guy on *Inside Out*, but it's usually not that simple. Anger is easy, and it feels validating and righteous, but what's underneath it? Are you hurt? Are you scared? Don't forget to validate those feelings too.

Ask yourself these questions:

1. What if I had it on the highest authority that those people are doing the best they can? (What does that do to your heart?)
2. What if I really knew all their struggles right at this moment? (Does that soften your sharp edges?)

Remember, it's not about them—it's about how believing they're doing their best will affect you. And if you can, friend, if you're ready, choose to believe it.

They're doing the best they can. It's time to release them.

CHAPTER 9

I'M SCARED OF SNAKES, PORTA POTTIES, AND BEING GHOSTED

A Recipe for Overcoming Our Fear of Rejection

> Find a group of people who challenge and inspire you. Spend a lot of time with them, and it will change your life.
> —Amy Poehler

The first person who broke my (Amy's) heart wasn't a boy. It wasn't a boyfriend. It wasn't a crush. It wasn't unrequited love. It was my best friend.

Her name was Monica. (I obviously changed her name because I'm not here to blast anyone, and I changed it to Monica because *Friends* is playing as background noise. I don't even know anyone named Monica.) We were fourteen, I think—freshmen in high school. Maybe sophomores.

I honestly don't know exactly how old we were. It doesn't

matter, and I honestly don't know what event caused our relationship to crumble. Maybe there wasn't an event at all. Maybe it was just a gradual fading away. Her slowly taking steps back, me desperately holding on to her even tighter until the string tying us together finally had so much pressure on it that it just snapped. If there was a confrontation, or major problem, or any kind of big dramatic event, I can't recall one. It's been too long, but Monica was my person. That much I remember.

From kindergarten through elementary school and through junior high, we were inseparable. Joined at the hip. Bonnie and Clyde. Two peas in a pod. Were we unhealthily codependent? I mean . . . it's possible. Would I go back and change things? Absolutely not a single second of it.

Except for maybe that one time I was making macaroni and cheese at her house and I almost caught the kitchen on fire. Or that time I spilled fingernail polish all over her bathroom floor. Her parents weren't thrilled about that one, but they loved me like I was their own.

Or that time we were making sugar cookies and I somehow got my finger stuck in the handheld mixer. How? Who does that? Why am I the way that I am? I just stood there, hovering over the ceramic bowl of dough, crying that my finger was going to fall off while Monica very literally ran around the house in a panic, yelling and screaming until her teenage brother came out, called us idiots, ripped the cord from the socket, shook his head, and walked quietly back to his room. Yeah, I would have probably changed that. We couldn't even eat the cookies because of blood and dead skin and unsanitary stuff. Good times.

During the school year, it was rare for a weekend to pass without us hanging out. During the summer, it was rare for a single day to pass without us hanging out. One summer we watched *Billy Madison* on repeat for an entire month. Let me just tell you that yes, that's a lot of Adam Sandler being very Adam Sandler-y, and yes, it was mildly inappropriate and I don't think we understood every joke, but we loved it. We soaked it up. The penguin scene and the scene where that kid pees his pants and Billy comes to his rescue—we reveled in it.

Vacations—we did them together. Sleepovers—we had too many of them to count. To know me was to know Monica and to know Monica was to know me. We were really close for a really long time, and when you're young you just trust. Before you've known regret, before you've been scarred, before you've been burned, before your secrets have been shared and your insecurities have been exposed, before your precious innocence has been taken from you and been traded in for a mix of awareness and knowledge with maybe a dash of bitterness, you hand trust out freely. Here! You have a little of my trust. And you have a little of my trust. And you, well I know you really well, so you can have all of my trust.

And that's how heartbreak usually happens, isn't it?

You trust somebody. They hurt you. Maybe intentionally. Probably not. Either way it doesn't matter because your heart still shatters all the same. And it gets put back together, but it's never quite the same way as it was before. Every heartbreak causes a person to be reborn.

Now listen. Please believe me when I say that I'm not angry at Monica. I wasn't even angry at Monica as an immature, knows-nothing-about-nothing fourteen-year-old. I understood that she wanted to walk down a different path than I was walking. I kind of wanted to stay in the same place I had always been in, and she wanted to try something new, so I wasn't mad at her. I didn't blame her.

I was just sad. Really, really sad. I wanted to continue doing life with her. I wanted to be her person, and she didn't seem to want those same things from me, and that is painful. Rejection cuts us to our core. But it's part of life. I don't think any of us get through without experiencing it at least once or twice.

So we take these pains and these struggles and these disappointments and these little cracks, and we fill them with something new. Hopefully we fill them with good things. Things like knowledge and compassion. Resiliency. And once we make it through these hard things, once we come out still breathing on the other side, we take out our pens and our paint and our glitter, and we fill those cracks with confidence. A confidence that's creative and colorful and really hard to shake. A confidence that's all ours, and we own it. And suddenly, before we really know what's happening, we aren't just surviving—we are actually living.

And unfortunately, sometimes we fill in those cracks with things like fear, anger, self-doubt, and self-loathing. We fill them with a severe lack of faith both in others and in our own ability to differentiate safe people from those who will eventually burn us. Or hostility toward those around us.

We shore up walls so high that nobody and nothing can break through. And we think these walls keep us protected. We think they serve as a barrier between negative feelings and our hearts, and they do. Those walls guard us well, but while they may defend us from the bad stuff, they also stop the good stuff from reaching us.

They keep us from feeling the sting of rejection and the pain of being unchosen and unwanted, but they also keep us isolated and alone. They seal our fate and they block us from the joy of laughing so hard our stomach hurts and our eyes water while sitting with a friend over appetizers at a favorite restaurant. They shield us from the fulfillment of true connection, separated from the bonds of sisterhood, and those walls stop us from the one thing our souls yearn for most of all—belonging.

I mentioned it in *I'll Be There (But I'll Be Wearing Sweatpants)*, but I think it's worth mentioning a second time. (Plus, it will help me get my word count up, which will make my editor very pleased.) In the last few decades, the number of Americans who believe they don't have close friends has nearly tripled. And according to data from a General Social Survey, when people were asked how many confidants they have, the most common answer was none.[1] None. Zero. Not a single confidant.

Those findings wreck me. I will spend my entire life trying to find a solution, because I simply can't let things stay the same without at least searching for a solution. I can't accept the status quo and I can't let the next generation suffer because we weren't brave enough to figure this out. Why are things like this? How did we let this happen and how do we fix it? These questions haunt me.

It's easy to blame social media, and sure, there's probably something there, but we were trending in this direction far before MySpace was ever a thing. MySpace. Bahaha. Oh, I cringe at the way I used to stress over choosing the song for my profile, and don't even get me started with that top-eight list. It's too much. I can't. I die. (If you're under the age of thirty-five, you probably are not familiar with the MySpace reference, and I apologize. Just let me be middle-aged for a second and keep on reading.)

We could blame our busy schedules and our endless pur-suit of the hustle, and we probably should. They are absolutely one of the major culprits at play, and we all need to be carefully rethinking the places we are investing our time and energy. Some people would argue that we've simply become a selfish, spoiled culture. While maybe we do tend to place ourselves at the center of things and demand that everyone revolve around our feelings and expectations, I will always believe the majority of people are wonderful, giving, and would help their neighbors if push came to shove. There are too many stories of kindness taking place to believe otherwise, so I'm going to refuse to indulge in that debate. I love people too much and have too much overall faith in humanity. Always have. Always will. Probably.

The point is that all this questioning eventually led me to this hypothesis: Perhaps at least a teeny tiny sliver of the problem at hand is that so many of us have been so repeatedly and woefully rejected, in one way or another, that we all collectively decided life was safer without the risk of deep friendship. We traded in authenticity for pretending, and we handed over our desire to be seen, known, and loved while picking up this counterfeit desire to merely be popular instead. Maybe we decided we didn't even need to be popular—we could settle for being invisible. Saying no to invitations. Hiding out in our homes. Blaming the world around us.

We gave up on rich conversations. Because in a rich conversation, you might accidentally be vulnerable. You might reveal too much about yourself. You might learn too much about the other person and form an attachment. You might show your cards. That didn't feel safe so we stopped, and then we started complaining that we were exhausted by meaningless chitchat. We grumbled that people were shallow and we started looking down on everyone around us.

We foolishly convinced ourselves we didn't need anyone and that the only person we could ever truly trust was ourselves, and we built our own little prison. Too tough for anyone to break through. Too strong for us to break out of. We took our fear and our insecurity and we masked it with pride, and we dared anyone to get past our bulletproof security system.

Again, this is just my hypothesis, and I probably would never have come to this conclusion if it wasn't for a girls' trip to Nashville a few years ago.

Four of us decided to go. We had been hanging out sporadically for a little while. We were definitely building something, but the foundation hadn't fully formed yet, ya know? So we went. We bought matching Dolly Parton shirts. We stayed at a nice hotel. We rode in an obnoxious pink limousine. I regret none of these decisions, because when in Nashville. . . . Plus, we were too lazy for the pedal taverns. Paying money to use my own body to get from point A to point B is a solid "nah" from this girl. I'm either going to walk for free or I'm going to pay for a ride. Anything outside those two options sounds expensive and exhausting and I am not here for it.

It was a great trip. From the first day to the last day. Everything was wonderful.

We talked a lot about what we were looking for in life. We opened up about wanting meaningful friendships, but how it takes work and intentionality and commitment to get there. We got to know each other on an entirely new level. We shared a single bathroom and we shared clothes and we learned which one of us snores the loudest and which one of us has a regularly scheduled bowel movement. There were some good conversations, some really good food, and some really hilarious pictures.

On the last day we decided to get matching tattoos, which was wild to me, but I was all the way in. I'd always wanted a tattoo but was too scared to get one. I didn't make a lot of "mistakes" growing up. I didn't color outside of the lines. I didn't push the limits. I didn't have a rebellious bone in my body. Plus, there was also part of me that secretly hoped maybe I'd marry Prince William, and I didn't want to ruin my chances by being inked up. Never mind that I can't keep a straight face during serious functions, my love for pants with a drawstring, and my lack of understanding which fork to use at fancy restaurants. Also my hatred of fancy restaurants or anything overly formal.

I'm the last in line to get the tattoo and right before it's my turn, I begin to uncontrollably sob. I'm talking buckets of tears, so much so that my false eyelashes fell right off. I tell the girls I can't do it. They surround me with hugs and encouragement. They reassure me they will still be my friend with or without the tattoo, but they ask what I'm scared of. At first, I'm not really sure. I was thirty-seven, so I was only a little scared that my parents would be mad at me. It was something else . . .

Ahhh, and there it is. The truth bubbles to the surface and explodes out of my giant mouth. "I'm scared I'm going to get this tattoo and y'all will leave me. I'm scared this friendship will end. They never seem to last, and I don't want to get friendship-dumped by y'all somewhere down the road. I think most people like me better in the rearview."

More hugs take place. More encouraging words. More reassurance. No annoyance (except from maybe the tattoo artist. Pretty sure I was not his favorite client that day.) No judgment. Just understanding and openness.

I take a deep breath, slowly exhale, and decide to go for it. I know I'll regret it if I don't. I decided that yes, the tattoo was a reminder of our friendship, and yes, the tattoo was a reminder of the memories we created and the bonds we formed, but more than anything else, it was a reminder of me getting over my fear. It was a reminder that I did a hard thing that day, that I took a leap of faith.

I lay on the chair, the tattoo artist stuck a fruit punch–flavored

Dum-Dum in my mouth so I'd stop wailing, and I've never looked back. That tattoo can't be taken away and neither can those memories or those lessons learned.

But that experience got me thinking about the fear of rejection. Maybe I wasn't the only one who wrestled with it and who felt held back by it. Fear is hard to destroy. To some degree we actually need fear in healthy doses. It keeps us safe, so I'm not suggesting that you ignore fear altogether. I'm suggesting that you manage it, reframe the way your brain processes it, and come up with little mind-shifts that will help you to continue moving forward.

It's normal that when we invite someone to lunch and they say no, we feel rejected and pull back. It's normal that when we initiate contact with someone and they don't respond, we pull back. It's normal that when we open up to someone and they don't return our vulnerability, we pull back. These rejections all feel like doors are slamming in our faces, and doors closing isn't especially pleasant.

But what if we stopped thinking of those experiences as closed doors and instead started thinking of them as gifts we've dropped off on people's front porches? Little gifts that say, "I like you. I'd like to be your friend. I think you're worth the time and the effort. You are safe with me, and because I've given you this gift, you can trust that you won't be rejected by me."

What if we made it our mission to hand out as many gifts as possible? What if we stopped assuming that just because the invitation to coffee didn't work out one specific time with one specific person, something is inherently wrong with us and we should stop reaching out to everyone altogether? What if we didn't hold the past close to our heart, and what if we didn't use it as a reason to not give friendship another go? What if we stopped looking at being told no as a door closed and instead started seeing it as a gate of connection being opened?

Seriously. To invite someone is a gift. To include someone is a gift. To ask them to hang out is a gift. To check on someone is a gift. To initiate a conversation with someone is a gift.

I won't lie to you, not all gifts are well received. Some get tossed aside and some are never opened, but that's not your problem. Your job is to give the gift. How it gets handled after that is up to the other person, but you can rest easy because your heart was in the right place.

I'm not saying we give our gifts out to anyone and everyone. I'm not saying that we are unwise, unaware, or foolish. That's exhausting. It's essential that we learn to notice the people who are choosing us, and it's essential that we learn to hold on to the people who are holding on to us.

I'm simply saying that we can handle a little rejection from time to time. We don't have to be shaken or humiliated by it. A failed attempt at friendship does not make you a failure. A friendship that gets lost does not make you a loser. If we are all on the search for our people, then we can all expect to also find the people who weren't made for us along the way. It's part of the journey.

Fear of rejection is a limiting belief. Limiting beliefs hold us back from so many things, including deep and meaningful friendships. They are barriers between who we believe we are and who we really want to be. After Monica rejected me as a teenager, I think I started to believe that everyone would eventually reject me as well. This became the story I told myself. I told myself that I was easy to leave, that I was a rearview mirror friend, because maybe I looked better standing in someone's past. Those fears became a part of my identity, stuck with me for a long time, and kept me stuck. I just never realized it until that trip to Nashville. Overcoming my fears was a big deal. It was empowering. It was life changing.

The Good

With God on your side, you are absolutely capable of overcoming your fear of rejection.

The Bad

Rejection really does sting, and our past does have a way of limiting the things we believe are possible in the future. Most of us have scars. Most of us have very real hurts from our childhood that we have brought along into our adult lives. Facing our fears and reframing the way we think about rejection isn't easy.

The Takeaway

Most of us are scared of rejection to some degree and most of us have been held back by it in one way or another. Sometimes that mindset makes us assume our friends will eventually abandon us, or it makes us push people away before they get the chance to reject us first.

If you're terrified of rejection, here are the six best things you can do:

1. Acknowledge your fear and your feelings.
2. Reflect on the way they're holding you back from the relationships you really want to develop.
3. Be gentle with yourself. Things take time to unlearn, and going in a new direction takes time and practice.
4. Pray a lot. Pray. Pray. Pray. Pray. Pray. God doesn't want you to be held back. He doesn't want you to live tucked away. He wants you to live a free and fruitful life. He wants you to be giving and open with others. This fear, it's not from him.

5. Shift your way of thinking. Look on all you have to gain by persevering.
6. Do it scared. The more you reach out, the more organic doing so will become, and soon you won't even have to think about it.

If we can learn to push our fears aside, we can open doors of connection between us and other people. We can be safe spaces for them. Every invitation we send, every conversation we begin is a gift we can give, and the more gifts we give, the more friendships we are likely to receive.

I can't think of a better way to be remembered or a better way to make an impression on someone's life than to be the one who made them feel valued and embraced for who they are.

CHAPTER 10

WHO EVEN AM I AND WHAT IN THE WHAT IS ACTUALLY HAPPENING?

A Recipe for Self-Awareness

> Self-awareness takes work. . . . It's not for
> everyone. Just for those who would rather be
> happier than right.
> —Neil Strauss

I (Amy) have gotten extremely—possibly even overly—comfortable going out in public looking like fresh dog doodoo, but once upon a time I actually knew a thing or two about makeup and hair and fashion. I worked in boutiques for years and I cared about my appearance. A lot.

However, let's all take a minute to stop and wave goodbye, because that ship has sailed far, far away, my friends.

The best advice I have nowadays is to keep a pair of tweezers in the car with you at all times. Because at a certain age rogue facial hair happens. At least for me. It happens on my chin. It happens on my neck. It happens along my jawline. It happens when

I'm driving along minding my own business and brush a hair out of my face only to realize that's not a head hair, it's a face hair that's come to live here in all its unwelcomed glory. Excuse me, sir, did I say you could occupy my land?

It's like my eyebrows got tired of having so many close neighbors, so they migrated down my face where they could spread out and have some extra land to roam free. Maybe grow their own garden and have some farm animals. Just really living their best life on my face. Getting older is fun. You just never know what's going to happen.

I swear I look in the bathroom mirror every morning for these hairs and I almost never find them. Then I get in the car and *sur-priii-iiise!* There they are.

Maybe they are growing during the forty-five seconds it takes me to walk from my bathroom, out the front door, and to my car. I honestly don't know for sure. Or maybe sunlight just has a sneaky way of telling the truth—of revealing things we can't otherwise see in spaces and places that hide the real light. There's no light for chin hairs like car light, and there's no light for bikini line hairs like the light that exists when you're already at the beach in a swimsuit. Lord, help us.

About five or six years ago, when I was at one of my loneliest points, I was desperate for good friendship. I was starving for it, like a withered-up plant that's been without water for months. I remember sitting on my kitchen stool feeling unbelievably sorry for myself. I was ready to give up completely. *I guess this is my life now. Me, myself, and I* (and obviously these chin hairs).

I'd found myself in this pattern where I would become incredibly close with one group of friends, then I'd eventually find out that the closeness wasn't felt on both ends (I'll get to that). But for my part, I'd genuinely believed I'd found my people. And then after a year or so of feeling like I was firmly in the center of the circle, I'd find myself being pushed to the outskirts. The B-list friend yet again. Easily discarded like the extra salt and pepper packets you get in the bottom of a fast-food bag.

After this kept happening back-to-back, I was up to my ears in questions and without any answers. I had shown up. I had been fun. I had loved well. I had done every single thing I knew to do and I was left alone again and again and again.

In my mind it made zero sense. The only logical explanation is that people were mean—allllll the people, every single one of them. Friendship was a load of garbage, and going through life friendship-less, people-less, and village-less was simply my lot in life. These were the cards I was dealt, and it was my job to accept them with a brave face and move along.

Sometimes I think good things happen when you're at the end of yourself (and your own capability) and at a complete loss. You can't figure it out anymore and you're about to give up when you're suddenly given a gift of understanding. It was in this moment of thinking the worst of other people that I learned about the locus of control theory.

"Locus of control" is a term coined by Julian B. Rotter in 1954. It refers to the amount of control an individual believes they have when it comes to their own behavior, their own success/failure, and their overall life experience. There are two forms of locus of control: internal and external.

Internal: People with a high internal locus of control see themselves as having a large amount of self-control over their attitudes, their perspectives, and their outcomes. Because of this, they are more likely to take ownership for things that happen in their life. An example of this might look like someone thinking, *I really nailed that presentation because I worked hard at it and studied the material well.*

External: People with a high external locus of control see themselves as having a low amount of self-control over their attitudes, their perspectives, and their outcomes. Because of this, they are more likely to reject ownership for things that happen in their life. An example of something a person with a high external locus of control might think is, *Huh. That presentation went really well. I bet those two cups of coffee I had really made a big difference in how I performed.*

I know these are some big psychological terms, but they changed things for me in a major way. It was exactly what I needed to hear once I was ready to hear it. I realized that I had blamed everyone and everything for the way those friendships went down, and I never looked in the mirror and truly examined what I could have done differently. I saw myself as powerless, weak, and without hope when it came to my friendships. And I realized this wasn't okay.

Can I tell you something and be really honest? It's very vulnerable and scary to truly look in the mirror when things are going wrong in our lives. What if we find out we're awful? What if we find out we're just not even likable? Or scariest of all, what if we're not capable of change? It's a whole lot easier to be offended and cast blame than it is to self-reflect. It feels good, it feels validating, it feels safe. But guess what? It's never going to get us to where we want to go because we have zero control of others. Zero, zilch, nada. That means we have exactly one way to change things: working on ourselves.

I didn't love the way things in the friendship department of my life were going. Things were clearly being mishandled by the management, and I decided it was time to change my belief system. I refused to continue to believe that I was a victim in all this. I decided to get real comfortable facing my own music and calling myself out on my own mess.

And yeah, I knew that the other players in this friendship breakup weren't exactly spot-free or blameless or anything, but blaming them hadn't done anything to help my situation because I also knew that I couldn't change their behavior. I couldn't change the way they operated, so my only option at this point was inner work. I'd tried everything else, so why not give this a shot?

For months I learned everything about myself.

I took personality tests. I read books. I went to therapy. I cut out distractions and noise. I listened to the things my closest family members had to say about me, which was hard by the way. I worked at not getting defensive when they had feedback, ugh. I didn't make excuses when they offered kind evaluations and caring criticisms. And listen, I typically hate being criticized. Like . . . I really hate it. I knock it down, roundhouse kick it in the face, avoid it like a toddler avoids broccoli on their dinner plate, and then go hide in a pillow fort somewhere where its echoes can't hurt me.

But I knew it wasn't healthy or wise to continue to build house after house with the exact same structural flaws either. There was a continual problem and I was the common denominator. I was too old at this point. Too tired of playing pretend in my friendships and too tired to go back to the same ol' same ol'. I wanted something that was made to stand. Something that was made to stay. Something that was made with some integrity, strength, and longevity.

So I researched and I journaled and I asked really tough questions and I got really real with the answers I provided. It was hard work. It was messy work. It was essential work. Self-awareness usually is.

But I refused to live alone. I refused to give up on friendship. I refused to let down my past self, the one who dreamed of belonging and doing life with people. I couldn't let her down and I couldn't settle for a life that was less than I was made for. Couldn't do it. Wouldn't do it.

Growing isn't an especially easy thing, but I'm so grateful I forced myself into it.

During the process, here are some things I learned about myself.

My people-pleasing wasn't cute. And it wasn't just "being nice." It was a problem, and it caused me to constantly abandon myself, to force myself into boxes where I did not fit, and to hide some of the more honest parts of myself so that I could be pleasing to all. I wanted to be liked by everyone when what I needed was to be accepted by a few.

Ignoring confrontations wasn't healthy and it didn't make my friendships stronger. I thought I was being easygoing, but in reality, pushing my frustrations down only led to these feelings leaking out in passive-aggressive ways.

I took everything way too personally. People didn't think about me nearly as much as I thought about me. Most of the time they weren't purposefully leaving me out. They weren't sitting there whispering, "Eww, let's not invite her." I simply wasn't on their radar. Their lives didn't revolve around me—and weren't supposed to.

I was very thoughtful and always took other people's feelings into consideration, I didn't always take my own feelings into consideration, and that was actually important.

I assumed people would eventually not like me, which led me to constantly look for clues that they indeed didn't like me, so that I could push them away before they got the chance to do it.

I was capable of far more than I gave myself credit for.

I didn't hear what people said. I only listened so I could jump in with a clever, funny, charming response when I should have listened to understand them better.

I was strong when it came to making initial connections and conversations, but my energy petered out.

I was on my phone too much. I spent too much time when I was with people looking down at my screen instead of making them feel that they held and deserved my attention. I was so busy connecting with a device that I forgot to connect with the beautiful human sitting right in front of me.

My insecurities kept me constantly looking inward. I was so consumed with putting myself down that I wasn't coming up for air often enough to lift other people up. I was so focused on being humble that I didn't even realize how self-absorbed I'd become in my insecurities. That inner critic had robbed me of some relationships.

I was so scared of hurting people's feelings and of being unliked that I shied away from being honest.

I was drawn to fun friends. I was drawn to exciting friends. I was drawn to good-time friends, which is awesome. But I was also drawn to fickle friends, and friends who didn't know how to stick through the hard stuff. Friends who would tell you what you wanted to hear and not what you needed to hear, just for the sake of keeping things surface-y.

———

I can't even begin to tell you how much confidence I gained during this time of self-reflection. I was always scared that uncovering my flaws would ruin me, but it actually built me up. Owning who I was in every facet gave me a strength I'd never known. I knew who I was. And for the first time in maybe forever, I kinda liked me.

I felt like I had things to bring to the table and I was comfortable in my own mind, in my own feelings, in my own jean size, and in my own heart. And it was all like coming home, snuggling up in a warm bed, and resting well.

I promise, you can handle the kinks and the nicks that come with self-awareness. With growing. Owning who you are won't break you. Continuing to ignore it might.

You'll dust off pieces of yourself you never knew existed, and those pieces will absolutely shine with a little polish. You'll uncover things that aren't the best, but once they're uncovered and addressed, they can be dealt with. You'll know your strengths and your weaknesses. And you'll learn how to use them both to get to where you want to be. You'll know the parts of you that make you a good friend, and when you mess up (and you will mess up), you'll be able to take full responsibility and say, "That's something I'm working on. I will keep doing better."

Losses will still sting, but not to the same degree because this time, you'll have you. You'll know you. You'll embrace you.

We can't constantly be looking at ourselves in the dim, flattering light of the bathroom or the harsh, insulting, fault-finding fluorescent light of run-down department stores either. They both serve a purpose. They both have their place. But they both lie a little too.

We have to get used to looking at ourselves in the truth-telling light of the Son. That's where we'll find our weird chin hairs. And once we find them, we can decide whether to pluck them or accept them and let those bad boys be.

The truth is, those flaws I have are equally partnered with the things that make me *me*. I genuinely care about people, I'm comfortable putting others first. The growing didn't change who I am—it made me stronger. I'm more confident than ever when it comes to friendship, because I know me. I truly, truly know me—the good and the bad. And I own it. Every single bit. What an utterly gorgeous gift when we can identify an issue and say, "That's on me." And what an equally gorgeous gift when we can identify a strong point and say, "That's on me too."

I'm an absolute catch, and you are too. It doesn't matter that you have things to work on (we all do!). Those chin hairs don't disqualify you—we all have them, but few people will take the time to self-reflect and pluck them out.

No matter what happens, the experience of self-reflection and self-work empowers us, and when we feel empowered, our lives change. And when our lives change, doors start opening everywhere for the right people to come inside.

The Good

Self-work is like eating your vegetables and getting some fresh air when you're having a bad day. It doesn't always sound fun to go on a walk or make a salad, but the rewards are worth it. And yes this is "the good." The good is that we are *empowered*. We are *empowered* to grow and transform and do better.

The Bad

Fear is powerful, but it isn't too powerful, I promise. We have to stop being afraid to do the work, or if we can't shake it then just do it scared. Take a deep breath—nothing you're going to see is going to disqualify you from being an incredible human being worthy of connection. You've got this.

The Takeaway

What does it look like for you to face yourself fully in the mirror?

1. Start by self-examining.
2. Next (and this is going to require bravery) ask someone who knows you well if there's something they see in your life that you could work on.
3. Take a deep breath. You're not going to die from the truth. In fact, they say the truth sets you free, so be free, friend.

ESSENTIAL INGREDIENTS FOR
FRIENDSHIPS YOU CRAVE

Just like you're never going to be able to make queso without cheese, there are also a few essential ingredients to cooking up solid friendships. Have we gone too far with the queso references? Are you tired of them at this point? That's too bad because we love a good theme and it's our book, so we're going to keep pouring them out like . . . well, like queso.

<u>CAPACITY</u>

Every one of us has a different capacity for friendship. It depends on how demanding your job is, how many kids you have, and other factors such as how many close family members you have. (If you're really close to your sisters, your capacity might be different than someone who is an only child.) There is no right amount of capacity to have and there is no wrong amount of capacity to have, but someone with a large capacity for friendship—with an abundance of time and energy to give— might find it frustrating to become close to someone who has a small capacity. We can be there for each other when times get tough, but I've found it extremely beneficial to pour my time and energy into someone whose capacity and desire for friendship are similar to mine. Our capacity will wax and wane over the years. It won't always be fifty-fifty, but over the span of the friendship, the give and take should be about equal for things to be healthy.

RELIABILITY

Nobody is going to respond to every text. People have their own lives and as their friends, we have to both respect that and encourage them to be living well, ya know? Their lives can't and shouldn't revolve around us. However, in a solid friendship both parties should have a sense that they can rely on each other. That they can count on each other to show up when it matters most.

Reliability doesn't happen overnight. It isn't instant. It's like a castle; it takes time to build—brick by brick, layer by layer. Those texts you repeatedly ignore might not be a big deal, but they do send a certain message: *I am not always going to respond to you.* Those invitations you repeatedly decline might not be a big deal in and of themselves, but they do send a certain message: *I have better things to do with my time. I don't mind rejecting you.*

When your friend is in a crisis, when she really has an emergency or something major comes up, she's going to reach out to the people who have been there for the little things. She'll know they'll be here for her now because they were there for her then. Those calls. Those texts. Those little coffee dates. They all mean something. They all add up. They all build a foundation. Don't expect people to magically believe you'll be there for them when it really matters, because it *all* matters. I cannot stress this enough— *show up for your people.* Reliability is everything to a relationship.

APPRECIATION

Only we know what we're feeling. What matters to our people is how we actually live out those feelings in real time. Do you appreciate your friends but keep those feelings inside, or do you show your appreciation for them by investing in the friendship? By showing up? By loving them with your actions? By telling them you care? Nothing will make a person run from a relationship like being taken advantage of or like feeling they are unwanted, unseen, or easily discarded. Little acts of love go a long way here.

VULNERABILITY

We've said it before and I'll say it again: If you don't let your friends see the real you, they can't love the real you. They may want to, but if you're hiding and performing and smacking a smile on top of your struggles, you're keeping them on the outside and holding them at arm's length. You will struggle to feel belonging because you will know that you're keeping a part of yourself locked up and hidden.

It can be scary to let people in. It can be scary to let them know what's really going on. But that's the kind of stuff that real and satisfying friendships are built on. You can have a bazillion friends, but if you don't let any of them in, you're still going to be lonely. You don't have to share all of yourself all at once, but dip your toe in, see if it's safe, and then keep moving forward one brave step at a time.

(MANAGED) EXPECTATIONS

1. **Don't expect yourself to be the perfect friend.** Remember that you're human too! All you can do is try your best, learn from your mistakes, and stay humble.
2. **Don't expect your friends to be perfect** (because they're not). People are going to make mistakes—they're going to

say the wrong thing or do the wrong thing. Expect your friends to be human (because they are) and make room for it. Great friendships are built on having lots of grace for each other.

3. **Don't expect your friendships to never hit bumps.** Misunderstandings, confrontations, hurt feelings—that's all a part of it. Learn to expect it and not be afraid. It doesn't mean things are bad—a lot of times it means the opposite. Every time you get through something hard together and you come out the other side, you'll be closer.

PART 2

Recipes for Deepening Your Friendships and Doing Life Together

CHAPTER 11

SOO . . . IS THIS THE PART WHERE WE MAKE PLANS TO ACTUALLY HANG OUT? BECAUSE THAT WOULD BE COOL.

A Recipe for Transitioning from Acquaintances to Actual Friends

> How about "diamonds are a girl's best friend"?
> Nope. It should be switched around and pointed
> out, instead, that your best friends are diamonds.
> —Gina Barreca

There's this woman in my (Amy's) workout class. We know each other's names. We always say hi. We've had a few three-minute conversations before class, but that's it. I like her. I get good vibes when we interact.

But how—I'm sorry, *how*—do I go from acquaintances to actual friends without coming off like an absolute goofball? I would rather not accidentally present myself as a serial killer, and

I don't know how to approach someone else and just be like "Can I have your number? Can I text sometime? Will you be my friend, and can we eat cheese together in your kitchen sometime?"

It's weird, right?

The jump from "I know of you" to "I know you" is tricky and it's awkward. There's really no way around it. Yes, every once in a while it happens organically, but I believe with friendship, like with most things, you have to get out of your comfort zone. You have to take a leap of faith. And as someone who never wants to leave her couch or take off her sweatpants, I fully understand the fear of making this happen.

So instead of loading you up with tips and tricks and statistics and a bunch of mumbo jumbo, I'm simply going to tell you some stories of how my personal friendships jumped from merely acquaintances to actual friends.

I knew Amber. Years before, we had been on a few girls' nights out together in a big group. But in those in-between years, the group had dispersed and all communication between Amber and me had stopped. We had never had a one-on-one conversation. Group stuff, shallow banter, and "Hahaha, oh my gosh, I love your top. Where'd you get it?" conversation only.

One day, and it just happened to be during one of my lonelier periods in life, I was scrolling through Facebook and stopped at Amber's page. She had shared a deeply vulnerable post from her husband about recently finishing up a stint in rehab for alcohol and gambling addiction, and it tugged at me.

For starters, I admired his openness and willingness to share. Someone who is willing to expose their struggles, their burdens, and their truth in an effort to help others feel less alone is my kind of person. I also knew their world was about to get rocked.

We live in a fairly small town, and gossip tends to spread like pink eye through a preschool. I knew their social circle was about to change. I knew their weekends were about to change. I knew everything about their entire life was about to flip upside down and inside out.

I didn't know whether they wanted new friends or not. I had no clue. Like I said, it had been years since we talked, but something pulled at my heart.

Reach out.

Be there for them.

For hours, I debated back and forth with myself. Just a scrolling conversation in my own mind.

What do I do?

I don't even have her number.

Does she remember me?

Is she going to think I'm being intrusive or nosy? If I contact her, will it come across as pushy or needy? Is she being bombarded with messages right now?

What happens if she thinks I'm an idiot?

Finally, the tug became too strong to ignore, so I went for it. I mean, what did I honestly have to lose at this point? I was already lonely. I had cried just a couple of nights before to my husband and told him that if we were to pick up and move towns, I wouldn't even have anyone to call to tell. No going-away party. Nobody to help pack up. I didn't think anyone would care. They'd probably ask questions when they saw our house hit realtor.com, but nothing more than that.

We knew plenty of people, but it was just one of those empty times where our lives had a blank space when it came to friendship, which—let me just gently remind you—happens to everyone. We all get lonely. We all have transitional seasons where the leaves change and the temperature drops. It's part of life, so if you are feeling shame over your lack of a social circle, please take the shame, put pajamas on it, read it a bedtime story, and put it to bed for good. Shame helps nothing and hinders pretty much everything. Down with shame.

I decided that as long as my message to Amber was heartfelt and sent with pure intentions, I needed to send it. If she thought I was weird, so be it. I'll take being called weird for an act of kindness any day of the week. Slap that label on me.

I got her number from a mutual friend, and I proceeded to tell her how proud I was of both her and her husband; how I couldn't imagine the pain they'd both experienced but I could sympathize with them; how I would be praying for God to cover them with protection, strength, and mercy; and how neither my husband nor I cared about alcohol and would be happy to hang out without a drink, or even the thought of a drink, at any time.

And she responded. And from there we hung out casually. Our first meal was actually chips and queso on the porch at On the Border. Amber's friend Meg joined us. And from there our husbands and kids got to know each other.

It took time to build. It didn't happen overnight. I had to earn her trust because her walls were up. She'd been through too much to just let anyone walk right through her gates and into her home. I understood that and I also knew she was worth it. At least I hoped she was. I'd been burned so many times before. I felt like I could handle disappointment again, but I couldn't handle just sitting in my house alone, twiddling my thumbs, doing nothing to help myself or my situation. A failed attempt was better than no attempt at all.

And now, years later, Amber's the one I call. With the good stuff. With the bad stuff. With the dumb, nonsensical stuff. With the heavy stuff. With the light stuff. She's my errand friend. She's my emergency contact. She is one of my most precious confidants and my most trusted allies. She'd have my back through anything and I'd have hers.

And it all started with a text, a prayer, crossing my fingers, and taking a giant risk.

Sometimes I'll ask Amber what made her respond to me that day and what made her keep coming back. It would have been so easy to ignore my text completely or to reply with little hearts and then never talk to me again, so why respond to me?

And she always says, "Because you walked in when everyone else was walking out."

I'll never forget that. What a blessing it is to sit with someone when they're going through it and to stay when things get messy. Life will inevitably get real at some point, and we all need friendships that are real to get us through to the other side.

I (Jess) love Amber's story because it doesn't involve being a mom. Our kids didn't know each other. We weren't running into each other at school. It involved us, and the lesson of walking into somebody's life and choosing to stay applies to everyone.

It isn't exclusive to moms. It isn't even exclusive to women. It isn't exclusive to twelve-year-olds or sixty-five-year-olds. It isn't exclusive to one religion or one occupation. It isn't exclusive to a certain race, a certain income level, or a certain personality trait.

Friendship belongs to everyone.

However, for this section I (Amy) am going to focus on my mom friends. Please skip it if the topic of motherhood is a painful one for you or if it makes you feel disheartened in any way.

I wouldn't even include it except that learning how to become friends with my kids' friends is an essential part of my story.

If your kid is coming home talking about a kid on their team or in their class that they'd like to hang out with, this is the easiest, most organic way I can think of to make a connection between yourself and the other parent. It still takes a bit of a gamble, but it feels a little more natural to say, "Hey, my son is really having fun getting to know your son. I was reaching out to see if we should get them together sometime!" than it does to expose yourself.

It's good for your kid, and it's good for you. I see no drawbacks, losses, or setbacks here.

JENN

Jenn is another mom who is up at the school fairly regularly. We walked to pick up our daughters at the exact same time every day and we had mutual friends. The first time I met her, she made a slightly inappropriate joke that completely caught me off guard, and from then on, she had my full attention.

I am decently outgoing but I do have social anxiety, and I can definitely be awkward and introverted at times. But I still don't mind putting myself out there on occasion. I have a high capacity for friendship, so I am accustomed to making the first move. I'm accustomed to being the first one to make a playdate happen and being the one who reaches out. But with Jenn, it was a nice change of pace because she really made an attempt to be my friend.

She got my number from a mutual friend. She made sure I knew where the other teachers were hanging out during lunchtime when we would sub together. I noticed her efforts and, in my opinion, there's nothing more essential to friendship than effort. You don't have to be perfect. You don't have to be the funniest.

You don't have to have it all together. You don't have to say all the right things. Friendship rewards the ones who try. The ones who keep putting themselves out there, the ones who get back up after they fall down.

For once, it was nice to have a friend pursue me, so I put my focus and my attention into connection with Jenn.

LEAH

Same with Leah. She lightly stalked me on Facebook before sending me a message about our sons being in class together and from there, things bloomed. We went from Facebook messages to exchanging phone numbers. The friendship began with our kids, but it's more about us now.

Leah was genuine and showed up consistently, and it was all so refreshing. She was also honest, and that's a trait I've come to deeply admire in a person. For a while I looked for friends who were, let's say, pleasant. Friends who were a little more likely to tell you what you wanted to hear as opposed to what you needed to hear. I was insecure and fragile, and I honestly didn't want to endure anything even slightly confrontational or uncomfortable.

I didn't think I could handle it, but with time and reflection, I realized those pleasant friends were usually the first out the door when things got difficult. I realized they didn't come to me when I messed up or hurt their feelings. Instead of clearing the air between us, they were more prone to clear the entire relationship and leave me wondering what had gone wrong.

But Leah was easy to be around and supportive. She was someone I trusted, and it made it easy to begin a friendship with her. To this day I can't think of anyone in my contact list who is faster to show up when I need help or a laugh than Leah.

ELLIE

Ellie and I have kids who have been best friends for five years now. Her son is like an extra kid to me. I keep his favorite snacks in the pantry, and I know his favorite drink and his order from Wingstop, so Ellie and I have been in contact for a long time. But I'd say it's fairly recently that we've gotten close.

I tend to assume everyone hates me. (Unless they are overly obvious about not hating me, and even then I'll still randomly send a text and be like, "Are you mad at me?" And they'll be like, "No, why? Should I be?" And I'll be like, "No, you just haven't specifically told me that you're not mad at me in a couple of weeks, so I wanted to make sure." And they'll be like, "Amy, stop. You're out of control right now." And then I'll laugh and we will move on. I'm trying to get better, but when I say that nobody has ever managed to get all of their ducks to swim in a perfect line, I mean it. We're all a little quirky. We've just got to find the people whose quirks we can handle.)

So I do this thing where I assume people don't like me, and Ellie does this thing where even though she's awesome and beautiful and basically the best, she also worries about whether people like her, so it took us a while to upgrade past the acquaintance level to the friendship level. Friendship can't be cooked in an air fryer. It usually takes time to season, time to marinate, and then time to grill over low heat.

But Ellie took a risk and invited my husband and me to her wedding, and that brought us closer. Then her husband and my husband seemed to hit it off and that brought us closer. Then I took a risk and asked if she wanted to take golf lessons with me, and that brought us closer. Then she and her husband invited my family on vacation with them one spring break, and that pretty much sealed it. We all had a blast. It was so easy and so comfortable.

We've had so many discussions about struggling in social situations and feeling awkward a majority of the time and being unsure of ourselves. Little by little, moment by moment, step by step, we have built this beautiful friendship.

What will happen if our sons suddenly aren't friends anymore? What happens to us if they have a falling-out? I don't know. I hope that doesn't happen. I hope I get invited to Ellie's son's wedding one day in the distant future. I hope she asks me for pictures of them in kindergarten to put in the slideshow during the reception, but I am fully aware that it is extremely rare to be lifetime friends with anyone, so I guess we'll see. For today, I'm extremely grateful for Ellie, her husband, and her entire family. I will always steer my son to be a good friend to her son, but there's only so much I can control.

I hope these stories have illustrated how each friendship began because a risk was taken, a gamble was made. Someone has to initiate. Someone has to start. Someone has to invite. Someone has to press play. This is the only way any adult friendship is ever formed.

If we are all waiting around for someone else to make the first move, we all end up just waiting around.

My theory is that as girls, most of us were told that it was desperate to make the first move when it came to boys. You don't call them. They call you. You don't go to them. They come to you. You don't ask them. They ask you. You play hard to get, and this mentality has carried over into our adult friendships.

"If they really wanted me, they'd try," we tell ourselves as we stand with our arms crossed and wonder why we don't have any deep friendships. We expect them to go the whole one hundred, and we stand guard without so much as getting a toe wet until we know the waters are safe before we dive in. And it just doesn't work this way. Friendship will always require work on both people's parts. One person cannot do all the lifting.

Like I said, friendship rewards those who make the effort. It rewards those who keep going.

These are a few examples of times the friendship worked out, but let me assure you that for every friendship success, there are twenty friendship failures. You just can't give up. You may be safe inside, but you won't know the warmth of the sun until you're brave enough to open your front door and step outside. Friendship is worth it, and yes, you have what it takes to make it happen.

The Good

You are more than qualified.

Yes, you can be the one to host the party. Yes, you can be the one to say hi. Yes, you can be the one to set the wheels in motion, the one who consistently shows up, the one who initiates contact. Yes, you can be the one to stretch yourself, get out of your comfort zone, and learn new things. Yes, you can be the one to build the kind of friendship you've been dreaming of, but it's going to take a hammer, some nails, and a little sweat. It's not easy. Good things are rarely easy and easy things are rarely good. (Except for cheese in a can. Delicious—especially on Wheat Thins—and incredibly simple by design.)

Yes, you.

Today. Right now. With exactly what you have and exactly who you are.

The Bad

When I was growing up, we had a wood-burning fireplace for heat. On cold winter nights my dad would get that fire roaring, and it would become so hot in the living room you'd want to strip down to your bathing suit. It was like the actual surface of the sun. But wood heat means you're either on the surface of the sun or living in an igloo—there is no in-between. In the morning we'd wake up and the fire would have gone out in the night. I'd be all snuggled in my flannel sheets, and I'd hear my mom calling me to get up and get ready for school, except it was a cold and hateful world out there and I didn't want to. I'd burrow deeper, and my mom would call louder. Finally I'd rip it off like a Band-Aid and jump out of bed, pulling on clothes as fast as I could. That's what stepping out of your comfort zone to take acquaintances to friendships feels like sometimes. It's warm and cozy here, and the air is uncomfortable out there, but we gotta rip off the Band-Aid and just do it! There's a whole world of connection and belonging out there for us.

The Takeaway

Who do you want to take from acquaintance to friend? Maybe there's more than one person. Write down their names, and then jot down three things you can do this week to level up and get closer.

CHAPTER 12

TURNS OUT, YOU DO HAVE TO READ THE BOOK BEFORE YOU KNOW WHAT IT'S ABOUT

A Recipe for Being Less Judgmental

> Celebrate the people in your life who are there
> because they love you for no other reason than
> because you are you.
> —Mandy Hale

I (Amy) walked into my kids' school one especially chilly morning with my hair in some weird, messy bun. Did I look my best? No. Far from it. I went in there with my sweatpants on, having basically just rolled out of bed, but no biggie. I was dropping off one teeny tiny thing at the front desk, and then I'd be out of there before anyone could see me, right?

WRONG. THAT IS NEVER HOW THAT WORKS. NEVER.

I'm not sure what the scientific explanation is or if it has something to do with the way the stars line up or what, but that's never how it happens.

On the rare occasion that you are put together and dressed and feeling confident, you will see zero people you know. You'll go to all the hot spots, trying to be seen: Target, the grocery store, Starbucks. You'll even go inside instead of having your items delivered to your car. Still, you will see no one. But when you are looking disheveled and you are specifically hiding from people you know, they will find you. It's called the law of unattraction, I believe. Einstein wrote about it. Look it up.

Anyway, I'm in there, I'm about to leave, but before I can even turn around, I hear a surprised voice exclaim, "Amy, It's freezing outside! What're you doing out and about with wet hair?"

I look at my well-meaning, kindhearted friend and start cracking up. "Yeah, umm . . . my hair's not wet. I just haven't washed it in a while."

My poor friend. She felt awful for saying what she did. I bet she has apologized at least five times for it, which is totally unnecessary. I wasn't upset in the least. I wasn't embarrassed in the least. I found the entire interaction hilarious.

We've all been there. We've all been the one with the dirty hair. And we've all been the one who took our stupid, giant foot and stuck the whole thing in our stupid mouth. We've all jumped to assumptions, judged, and misinterpreted something.

I dunno. The older I've gotten, the more I've just come to realize that we all have our stuff. We've all fallen short. We've all messed up. We've all been on both sides of gossip—the side that spreads it and the side that the gossip is centered around. We've all been dramatic and we've all been the recipients of someone else's unwanted and unnecessary drama.

We've all done some incredibly idiotic things. We all carry baggage and old wounds that haven't properly healed. We've all reacted poorly. And unfortunately, whether we've tried to or not, we've all hurt someone we love. We've all handed out aches and pains and we've all received our fair share as well.

We're human, and we all have our stuff.

And we're all trying desperately to understand the world around us, draw lines from point A to point B, and make it all make sense, you know? We're all trying to distract ourselves from our own stuff so that we don't have to deal with it, distract others so they don't see it, and sometimes, for whatever reason, we do it by pointing to somebody else's mess.

"Here! Look over here! See their garbage! Let's talk about that because deep down, I'm terrified and insecure and broken over the junk going on in my own life."

But let me tell you, my own soul tends to be happier and more at peace when I don't obsess, stress, and completely engross myself with what someone else has going on, and I hand them lavish, unquestioning, undiscriminating love instead. My own heart is healthier when I walk slowly to conclusions about someone else instead of jumping straight to assumptions. My own mind is clearer, wiser, and quieter when I meet people where they are instead of expecting them to rise to my own egotistical expectations.

It's terrible to be judged, to feel the shame and the embarrassment of walking into a room that suddenly goes silent upon your arrival. It hurts to see eyes get wide and people start nudging each other with their elbows or see the hands cupped over mouths as secrets you know are about you get passed from person to person. Nothing feels more unsafe than a room where your problems, your struggles, and your private details are the open topic of conversation. Might as well chuck your heart right into a brick wall. That's pretty much what it feels like.

I remember one time when I was maybe three months into launching my Facebook page. I was a little tiny baby blogger, and I was sitting with a group of girls. I was really weird about the social media thing—still am, honestly. It makes me crazy uncomfortable. I don't actually love attention at all. I almost pooped my pants on my wedding day because I knew everyone would be looking at me walking down the aisle. Like . . . can we maybe skip the part where everyone is staring at me and go straight to stuffing our faces with cake and dancing? Okay, cool.

My biggest fear with social media was that people would think I was into myself, or they'd believe that I thought I was something special. And I didn't. I didn't at all. I was insecure and mortified to be putting myself out there. These were uncharted waters, and they were cold and choppy and I had no idea what to expect from the waves: Would they be the thing that brought me home or would I drown under the pressure? But I genuinely, with everything I had, felt like God was calling me to write. So I jumped into the writing world, fears and all—not because I wanted to, but because God told me to go.

As I sat with those girls, I said something like, "Oh, I don't know if I can go. I have an article due tomorrow that I need to write." I was scared to even mention writing, but I looked up and saw one girl make a smug face to another across the room. It wasn't the kind of face that can be misinterpreted. It wasn't a face I was supposed to catch her making, but I did. And it shook me.

People had clearly been talking about me after I'd gotten up from the table. They clearly had opinions and thoughts. And I was so close to quitting. So, so, so close to ending this journey before I got more than a few steps in.

I never brought it up. I never confronted anyone or discussed the situation to get clarity. Maybe I should have. I don't know what the right thing to do would have been, but I realized that group of girls wasn't a place where I could share successes or talk about work. It was a place I visited from time to time, but it wasn't a place where I made my home, so I let it be, created some strong boundaries, and did my best not to be harsh with them. After all, we've all got our stuff, right? Instant forgiveness seemed like the most peaceful option.

But going forward I've tried to make it a point to keep my judgments to myself or to squash them when I'm being unfair to someone. I'm definitely not perfect, or even close to it. This mouth, y'all. This mouth. And we all get carried away, but I don't want to be the reason someone

- quits on their dream,
- stops singing or gives up on a new passion project,
- stops posting about their job or feels like they can't celebrate their promotion,
- starts staying in when they used to love going out,
- suddenly goes silent when they used to love to share,
- hangs their head a little lower because their kid is having a hard time,
- feels like they can't open up about how they are going through depression, or
- feels like they can't be vulnerable when they are wrestling with their faith.

I want to be a safe space for others. I think most of us do, and in safe spaces judgments are shut up, assumptions are paused, and prejudices are pushed down.

We think we know everything. We think we have the whole story. We think we are aware of the full picture, but we usually know very, very little about what's actually going on in someone's mind and in their heart. It's like pretending we deeply connect to the lyrics of our favorite song when we've actually only heard the record in reverse.

Let's check on each other regularly and reach out, even when everything someone is posting on social media makes it seem like their life is sunshine and roses without a cloud in the sky. Because for all we know, they're going through a Category 5 hurricane and they just don't know how to open up about the storm that's raging in their life.

We don't know what others are dealing with. We don't know what they're carrying, and we have no idea what's happening behind closed doors. So let's ask questions directly to that person instead of making statements behind their back. Let's have conversations where the goal is true understanding and compassion instead of trying to find out what's going on so we can be the one with all the tea (which is, as far as I—a forty-year-old woman— understand, a teenage phrase for hot gossip).

Because the thing about spilling tea is that tea tends to leave a nasty stain on whatever it touches. Tea stains and words sting, and once the damage is done, it's done.

We can apologize. We can try to cover it up. We can try to smooth it out, but the wounds we leave others with can take up space in their heart for years to come. We can instantly demolish an otherwise healthy relationship that took a lot of time and effort to build.

So let's not compare. Let's not criticize. Let's not pull others down while hoping to lift ourselves up. Let's not judge. Let's not assume. Let's not make others out to be some awful villain when we don't know the whole story. Let's not worship them either.

They're only human. Maybe they're amazing, but there's a good chance they struggle too. I mean, we all do. No matter how it looks. We all struggle.

Let's not lack compassion when we have no idea the trauma they've walked through. Let's not be all "Well, what I would do is . . ." Because we aren't in their shoes. We've never been in their exact shoes. We have never, not for one single second, lived their life or known what the voices in their head whisper to them.

Let's not delight if they fall. Let's not clap if they lose. Let's not be smug or prideful. Let's not be envious of their life. Let's not be jealous. Let's not be ugly.

Just love them, accept them without judgment, and believe everyone is doing the best they can in life. It'll keep your relationships pure and, more importantly, it will keep your heart pure. And that's the only way we get through life.

The Good

God gave us brains. That's cool, huh? We can reason. We can draw conclusions. We can fill in the blanks, and we can often use these tools to keep ourselves safe.

The Bad

We can also use these tools to tear down others, criticize, and pass judgment.

The Takeaway

Humility goes such a long way. Yeah, other people have their stuff, but if we are self-aware and honest, we can admit that we do too. Sometimes when I find myself being judgmental, harsh, or going straight to assuming the worst about someone, I like to ask myself these five questions:

1. Is this judgment fair?
2. Is it helping me or anyone else to be taking this critical stance?
3. Is it possible my feelings are actually being led by insecurity?
4. Is it possible my feelings are actually being led by pride? (If so, remember, it's a long, painful fall from a high horse.)
5. Does my heart toward this person line up with Jesus' heart toward this person? (Oooof.)

Keep those questions in mind the next time you make quick assumptions about someone you don't know very well.

CHAPTER 13

WELL, THAT WENT OVER MY HEAD

A Recipe for Speaking Someone Else's _Love Language_

Love is something you do for someone else, not
something you do for yourself.
—Gary Chapman

My (Jess's) husband: Where do you want to go to dinner
tonight?

Me: I don't care. Anywhere is fine.

Him: Okay, Mexican?

Me: Nah, we just had Mexican.

Him: Want to do pizza?

Me: No, I'm not really in the mood for pizza.

Him: . . . .

Me: I'm not picky. I really don't care. Whatever is fine.
I'm down.

Narrator: But she was picky. She did care. "Whatever"
was _not_ fine and she was not "down."

S ometimes I really don't know what I want till someone says what I don't want out loud.

In 1992 counselor Gary Chapman proposed the idea of the five love languages in his bestselling book. He'd come to realize in facilitating couples therapy that one spouse often did not feel loved, even though the other spouse was convinced they were showing love in all the right ways.[1] Over the last three decades *The Five Love Languages* has become a tool for every kind of relationship, not just marriage. If you're unfamiliar with the five love languages, here they are:

Acts of Service
Gift Giving
Words of Affirmation
Quality Time (raises hand wildly)
Physical Touch (puts hand down quickly)

If you don't know what your love language is, this chapter will help.

My primary love language is quality time, and my secondary is words of affirmation (you usually have two, one being less important than the other). Many years ago I had a new friend who could almost never hang out. She was rarely available, and if we had plans, she'd often cancel them for one reason or another. The reasons always seemed valid, and we did see each other periodically (it just wasn't very much by my standards). It reached a point where I decided it might be time to just let the friendship go. I was sure she must not really like me.

The next time I saw her, she walked into my house and threw her arms around me. "Gosh, I just want you to know how important you are to me, and how much I value you. You are such a good friend, and I'm just so thankful for you." I was honestly shocked, but in a good way. I had an aha moment, and I started to realize how different this friend was from me. I'd expected her to have the same love language that I did, but she didn't. She wasn't telling me she didn't value me by canceling plans. She was just speaking love in a way I wasn't used to hearing.

Whenever someone tells me that their friends don't pursue them or prioritize them, my first question is always, "Are you sure they're not speaking in a language you're not accustomed to hearing?" Someone dropping off soup when the family is sick might just seem like they're "being nice" to you, but it might actually be them telling you they really love and value you as a friend. Someone's words of "You're the best!" might seem unimportant to you, but that might be them letting you know how much they care. The following is a list of the love languages, how each of those might look in friendship, and how you can learn to give and receive them better.

ACTS OF SERVICE IN FRIENDSHIP

This friend is always picking up after the party is over. Even when you resist and tell her, "Don't worry about it. I've got it," she just smiles at you like she doesn't understand these words you speak as she walks to the sink with a pile of dishes. When you're sick you might get a text from her that says, "I just dropped off a couple of things," and when you look out your door, it isn't a couple of things—it's actually forty-five different herbal supplements and a homemade meal.

She will take your kids while you have a doctor's appointment, and if she sits down on your couch next to the laundry pile, she'll probably start folding. She'll ask you if there's anything she can do to help you around the house and she will mean it. Reorganize your cupboards? Sure. Make the beds? Sure. Build you a new house? Sure.

One time I was staying at my in-laws' house and I offhandedly mentioned in front of my sister-in-law, Charis, that I'd forgotten my razor at home. She said nothing, but I kid you not, within thirty minutes there was a new razor on my bed. She is caring and servant hearted, quick to lighten your load whenever she can.

In a friendship that is more casual this might look like a text saying, "What can I do to help?" when you're sick or offering to pick up your kids after school. It might look like walking out of the room and coming back to find the friend quickly sweeping your kitchen or washing some pans. It might look like opening your game closet after your mother-in-law goes home to find it carefully organized from the cyclone it was before. *We have Skip-Bo? I didn't even know we owned that, it's been hiding in the pile so long.*

How to Speak Her Language

Look for things that you can do that would serve a practical need. Don't worry about doing everything, just do something. If you're not a great organizer (raises hand here), you don't need to offer to help organize the pantry, for example, but you could offer to grab groceries when she's not well, you could drop off a meal, or you could offer to watch the kids while she takes some time for herself.

How to Hear Her Language

Maybe she's hard to nail down for a girls' night or doesn't verbally express how much she loves you. Maybe she isn't very thoughtful with her gift giving, but notice the ways she is showing love and let it sink in.

GIFT GIVING IN FRIENDSHIP

When this friend gives a gift, she has thought it through. Remember that time two years ago you mentioned you might like a _____? You probably forgot but she did not, and now here it is, tied with a ribbon on your kitchen table. She is great at sending cards, which always inspires you to be better at sending cards. She picks you up little things here and there. "This mug made me think of you" or "I saw this shirt and I knew you had to have it." She is the one who comes up with the gifts that will make you bawl your eyes out. Like, "Here, this is a quilt I made from all your kids' onesies." Or "I got everyone who loves you to write you a note, and I put it together in this book." She is thoughtful and intentional, and she makes you feel seen.

In a more casual friendship this might look like bringing a dessert she heard you mention you liked to a gathering, or randomly sending you a few Starbucks dollars for a morning latte if she knows you had a late night.

How to Speak Her Language

First, try not to get an anxiety attack. If you're not a gift person it can be terrifying to try and reciprocate this language. It feels like they are the queen, and you are an actual idiot with no idea what to get. Maybe a candle. Wait, do they even like candles? Before you panic and buy a gift card to Amazon, take a deep breath. It doesn't have to be big, it just matters that it's thoughtful and unique to them. (Do not get them a generic "This is what I give to people for their birthdays" gift.) Try and pay attention to things they say when you're out together. Did they love that throw pillow at

Target? Sneak back and grab it for them. Are they always talking about how they can't find their favorite to-go mug? Go buy them a cute one. Don't wait for special occasions either. If you're at a shop and something looks like them, don't overthink it—just get it. Trust me, just the fact that you thought of them and got them something will speak volumes.

How to Hear Her Language

Try not to look at the gift they give you as an item, because it's much more than that. They were thinking of you in a very intentional way. Avoid saying things like, "You didn't need to get me that." They know they didn't *need* to—they want you to feel loved and thought about, so focus on that.

WORDS OF AFFIRMATION IN FRIENDSHIP

This friend is like having your very own personal cheerleader. The more expressive ones will have you feeling like a rock star every time you walk in the room. "OMG, you're so gorgeous! I love your outfit." They'll tell you all the things you never knew you needed to hear: "You're so amazing, you're the freaking best." "You're so incredibly talented!" "Girl, you got this, you're a queen."

If they're less verbally expressive, you might get a card that makes you bawl your eyes out, filled with all the things that they love about you. These friends understand the power of words and they use them for good. They'll speak life to your dreams, your soul, and every outfit you ever put on, and don't think they're just gushing—they mean what they say.

In a more casual friendship this might look like compliments out of the blue. She may not know you crazy well, but you're positive she's cheering for you. It might look like noticing when you do your hair different or get a new pair of jeans. These friends are professionals at encouragement.

How to Speak Her Language

Get good at speaking out loud the things that you love about her. Don't just write "Happy Birthday" on her card—dig a bit deeper and think about all the things that make her *her*. For your friends with this language, encouragement is like adding gasoline to her inner fire, and it goes a long, long way. You might think thoughts all the time about how great she is, just get good at verbalizing those thoughts.

How to Hear Her Language

Try not to be skeptical or dismiss what she's saying. She means what she says, even if it feels like too much. She's not just flattering you—she really thinks you're amazing and she wants you to know it.

QUALITY TIME IN FRIENDSHIP

This friend is the one to invite you to do things, or the first one to say yes when you ask her to come over. There are two subtypes in this language: one of them is conversation, and the other is activities.

Quality conversation: This friend really hears you when you talk to her. She is an amazing listener and gives you the gift of feeling seen and understood every time you process something with her. She doesn't just wait for her turn to talk (although she really likes to talk)—she listens in order to understand. She is really open about what she's going through. She wants you to be a part of her life and doesn't hold back when she's telling you what's going on. This friend loves going out to coffee or sharing a meal because there's uninterrupted time to connect through conversation. She may enjoy big groups, but it's important to also get undisrupted one-on-one time.

Shared experiences: This friend may love going to see a new movie together, because for her it's not about talking, it's about sharing an experience. She starts a lot of sentences with, "You know what we should do?" She might pursue Groupon for random activities or invite you to take a Pilates class. She wants to spend time together, but it doesn't necessarily have to be time face-to-face—it can be shoulder to shoulder. You might find her invitations random, but be open-minded. For her it isn't just about the activity. It's about doing it together.

In a more casual friendship this might look like her taking the time to ask you really good questions when you're at the same get-together. When you talk, you notice she's really listening to you. It might look like receiving random invites to events you've never even heard of before: Want to come to open mic night at Dave's? Want to try water Pilates with me? (Full disclosure: I don't know if that's a thing, but it probably should be.)

How to Speak Her Language

If it's quality conversation, get good at listening and also sharing. She wants to know about your life and what's going on with you. She doesn't want to just shoot the breeze—she wants to know you and be known. Ask open-ended questions (the kind that can't be answered with a simple yes or no), and be curious about what's going on in her life. Care about the things she cares about. For example, if she's excited about her new job, ask her about it. (Hint: She loves when you're real and vulnerable, so don't be scared to open up.)

If it's shared experiences, say yes to new activities and remember that while you're doing them, you're filling her up. When she invites you to a movie, it's not just a movie. If she asks you to come to a class with her, it's not just a class. To initiate, try inviting her to go ax throwing, to a concert in the park, or on a hike you heard about. She'll love it.

How to Hear Her Language

Maybe she's horrible at noticing the ways you could use practical help or giving compliments. Maybe she hasn't ever given you a hug. But pay attention to the gift of time that she's giving you and receive it for what it is: her love.

PHYSICAL TOUCH IN FRIENDSHIP

This friend gives lots of hugs. A hello hug, a goodbye hug, and a goodbye-again hug when she stayed five more minutes than she meant to. She might offer to give you a neck massage when you have a headache or put her hand on your shoulder when you're waiting in line. When you sit on the couch, she might sit right next to you rather than on the other five feet of available space. My love language isn't physical touch, but I am pretty affectionate. My friend and I went to a meeting one time, and I sat next to her on the couch. But what I saw as "next to her" she saw as "practically on top of her." I still laugh when I think about her leaning over and whispering, "You are on me. Can you scoot over a little?"

In a more casual friendship this friend might give you a pat on the back or touch your arm when she's talking to you. She might be a hugger, and you have to get used to the hello hug and the goodbye hug (insert my husband's entire family here). I can tell you as someone who has never been a physical touch person, I am now (with much practice) officially a hugger. I even like it now. (P.S. Hugs are proven to produce oxytocin, lower your heart rate and blood pressure, and even combat depression.[2] So apparently the huggers are onto something.)

How to Speak Her Language

If you're not comfortable with a lot of physical touch it can be hard to speak this one, but it's okay. Just do what feels comfortable to you. If you have to let her know that maybe the touching is too much (such as my friend telling me I was practically in her lap), just be gentle and remember that's how she gives and receives love. I have a friend who hates hugging and another friend who has physical touch as her love language. The first friend worked extra hard to get comfortable with giving and receiving hugs, and I thought that was such a sweet and intentional act of friendship. Did she ever enjoy the hugs? No, not really, but she made it about showing our other friend that she really cared.

How to Hear Her Language

Even if your idea of comforting someone is standing as far away as possible and using the tip of your hand to give a stiff pat on the shoulder with the obligatory "There, there," you can still work to recognize the hugs and shoulder squeezes for what they are: an action to show you how much you mean to them.

If you want deep sisterhood, it's so important that you learn to speak and hear the love language of your friends. Even if a certain love language is not natural or comfortable to you, it is learnable. You can scream "I LOVE YOU!" with your whole entire being, but if words don't mean much to that friend, they're never going to hear it in the way you meant it.

The Good

The love languages are an amazing tool to better understand each other. Now that you know the love languages (or have had a refresher), you can start thinking about what your friends' love languages might be—or just straight up ask them so that you know for sure. Filling each other's love tanks is essential to building deeper and stronger friendships.

The Bad

You can't just try and do your own love languages louder so your friends will hear—that's never going to work. You're going to need to speak their language. I don't know for sure, but I think even a whisper of what matters to them has more impact than a roar of what matters to you. If they love getting gifts, make it a goal to find something that makes you think of them this week. If they need to hear words of affirmation, try writing them a thoughtful card about what they mean to you. You don't have to do it perfectly (you're still learning), but don't give up before you even try. In the same breath, open your mind and heart to receiving love in different ways. If the way they love you doesn't seem obvious (you find yourself wondering, *Do they even love me?!*), try taking a step back and seeing if there's a way they're speaking love that you're not hearing.

The Takeaway

1. What is your love language? If you don't know after reading this chapter, try doing some research or taking an online test.
2. Think about each of the friends in your life that you want to go deeper with. Are there any clues to their love languages that you've noticed?

3. Even if you're pretty sure you've figured it out, ask your friends what their love languages are, and ask them if they feel loved by you. See where the conversation leads.
4. Make it a goal to do one thing this month for each of your closest friends that speaks directly to their language.

CHAPTER 14

WHAT IS THIS? THE TWILIGHT ZONE?

A Recipe for Breaking the Cycle of Bad Friendships

I really believe you are the company you keep and
you have to surround yourself with people who lift
you up because the world knocks you down.
—Maria Shriver

A couple of years ago a friend of mine and I (Jess) met up in
Las Vegas for a girls' weekend. She and I have been close
for a long time, but our relationship started as a big-sister, little-
sister relationship when she was in middle school and I was newly
married. I was a friend of her parents, and she and I used to go
out to coffee regularly. Now she's all grown up and our friendship has evolved, mainly because we can both have margaritas
and drive cars.

If I was ever wondering what it was like to travel with myself,
this was it. We are very similar, and our travel MO is identical.

Talk talk talk, coffee, talk talk talk, pool, talk talk talk, food, talk talk talk, more pool, talk talk talk, more food, talk talk talk. One of my more introverted friends says she feels tired just thinking about it.

I've never traveled with someone who is exactly like me before. I usually play a role, and that role is kind of about being oblivious but lots of fun. I'm really good at finding the next place to eat and not very good at remembering where my room key is. It's no worries, though, because my husband has it or my other friend has it.

After hours on the Strip eating, talking, laughing, and being merry, we decided it was time to drive somewhere for dinner. No problem. Both of us are amazing at finding good places to eat. Tacos? Burgers? Italian? Chinese? The world was our oyster. We didn't want to eat oysters, but still. You get what I'm saying. So we grabbed our purses, walked out the door, and headed to the parking garage that was about twenty levels high and just massive. I suddenly stopped and stared at it. My friend stopped too.

"Um. Do you remember where we parked?" I asked.

There was a long pause. "No. No, I don't."

I couldn't remember if I'd even parked in this particular garage. I was driving, but I was also talking, and I only remembered the talking. Because that's what I do. That's the skill set I bring: talking. Except the small problem was, that's her skill set too. We were both used to playing a role, and that role did not include remembering small details like parking spots.

With many prayers and thoughts of *What does one actually do if one loses their actual car in Vegas?* we finally found it (and we ate tacos because I know you were wondering).

The point is, sometimes we play a role in friendships without even realizing it. We do that with more serious things too. (Although my situation in Vegas was a little serious because it was, you know, my car and I was getting hangry.) I recently listened to a podcast that talked about relationships. The expert was explaining why we sometimes find ourselves in the same dysfunctional romantic relationships over and over again. She explained that it's not just simple attraction or chemistry—it's also finding a person we think fits us. If we're a puzzle piece, we'll look for the same "shape" of person to connect with.[1]

We're accustomed to playing a certain role and the important people in our life playing a certain role as well. That defining process can start as far back as childhood (think about the chapter on attachment styles). If we grew up with healthy relationships, then we already have an upper hand in connecting ourselves to healthy people. If we grew up with unhealthy relationships, we are preconditioned to be drawn to people who will play that same unhealthy role in our lives and subconsciously believe it matches with us.

I think it's exactly the same with friendships. Maybe you keep finding yourself in friendships . . .

- where you're the giver and they're the taker. You slip into a role of serving and loving, and eventually you realize that it's not going both ways.
- with narcissists, and you wonder what it is that attracts you to them in the first place. You always wonder why you didn't "see it" earlier.
- where the person gossips about you or betrays you in some hurtful way.
- with people who are perpetually disappointed in you. You

find yourself trying to please them until eventually you realize they're unpleasable.

- where they just don't value you as much as you value them, and it hurts.
- where they will tell you what they think you want to hear and won't be honest with you if they're upset about something.
- where you're tired of them ghosting you when you have no idea what went wrong.
- that are manipulative or just plain abusive.
- where the person is really "fun," but they disappear when the going gets tough.

When these friendships get tricky, or end, it's so easy to blame ourselves. It's so easy to automatically assume that we need to change, when in reality what we need to change is who we are surrounding ourselves with. Like a pilot who is having to adjust his landing destination, we need to learn to adjust the things we're looking for in a friend.

I'm not talking about when you've been hurt once, and so you tend to see everyone through that same lens, because that can happen too. It's easy to expect the worst and see the worst if you've experienced the worst, and if that's you, it's important to seek healing.

What I'm talking about is ending up in the exact same place on repeat. What I'm talking about is getting the exact same outcome like you've been driving for hours and somehow pull up at the same gas station you passed thirty minutes ago. If you want to get different results, you're going to have to use a different gear.

When I (Jess) was a kid, my dad would take me and my siblings on adventures in the woods. He'd tell us how important it was to bring a compass in case we ever got lost, and if we didn't have one, how to figure out our directions using the sun's shadow. He told us that if people don't use tools like that, they'll find that they keep circling back to the same spot over and over again. They don't even realize it until they somehow mark the tree they started at so that the next time they end up there, they recognize it.

If we don't have a compass, something to show us the way out, we'll keep finding ourselves landing at the same exact spot. Sometimes we work so hard to see only the good in people, and sometimes we work so hard to see only the bad in people. What we need to get better at doing is recognizing the truth in people.

It's easy for me to fall into the role of caregiving. I don't want to admit that, but it's true. I was raised by a pastor, and I learned that the way to love people is to serve them (and it's true—that is a good and important way). There are absolutely seasons when friendship calls for that. A friend of mine went through an extremely difficult time, for example, and it was an honor for me to step in and serve her in whatever way I could. That was loving her in that season. But caregiving is not friendship long term. Long term the giving has to go both ways, and there have been times I've forgotten that. I played the role I knew to play. The problem was that often the people who matched that side of me were looking for me to fill a need and weren't actually looking for mutual friendship. I did my best, but the results were always the same. They were left disappointed (because the needs were insatiable), and I was left feeling like a failure.

Over the years I've found friends who have given back, and they have helped reshape me. But I've also periodically found myself in similar dysfunctional friendships, and each and every time when the friendship started to combust, I felt like I was circling the same tree. How? How am I here again?

I have learned to not just fill needs because I can (or even because I want to), especially when I'm forming new friendships. I don't want that to become the foundation or expectation that I build friendship on. I still give because pursuit is important, but I pace myself. I'm naturally extra. I'm naturally extravagant. It's who I am. The goal isn't to change the core of who I am. The goal is to change the pattern of disappointing, unfulfilling, and empty friendships I've been experiencing. Sometimes, the truth is, our friend-picker is broken and it needs some adjustments and fine-tuning.

It's hard work, but I can do it, and you can too.

One last thing. It's going to be scary. When I stop playing roles I've always played, the fear becomes almost unbearable at times.

What if they don't like me? What if they don't want me? What if they think I'm a terrible person and talk badly about me to others? These things all happen when we break free of the box others have put us into. Humans like things that are tidy. We like things that are easy to explain and that "fit" into certain places. We put expectations on each other and on ourselves without even realizing it because it takes the guesswork out of things.

Oh. She is nice. I'll put her on this shelf.

She is super outgoing and always the life of the party. She belongs here.

She does not stand up for herself. She can go in this box.

People don't always want to know the whole of who we are. They want to know the bits and pieces of us they are comfortable with. The pieces they can neatly categorize. Sometimes they freak out a little when we show a different side of our personality. I've learned to show that side anyway. You cannot pick and choose to be friends with part of me, and I cannot hide who I am for this to work. None of us are required to be neat, orderly, and convenient in order to make others comfortable.

I think my deepest fear is that I'm going to find out that I actually am all alone. That's one of the many reasons I've fallen so easily into striving as a means to maintain close friendships. It's why I tiptoe and why I pretend. It's why I nod along with conversations I hate and it's why I still pretend to have no opinions when I actually have a lot of opinions. I'm just scared people won't accept that side of me, so I present the part that is easiest to digest. It's like when we burn one side of our kids' grilled cheese sandwich, so we flip it to the good side so they'll never know. (Don't act like you don't do it too.)

Stopping the cycle is terrifying. Letting go of friendships that are no longer healthy makes me feel sick to my stomach. But listen—and this is important—that's not a sign I should stop. I'm headed somewhere new, and it's going to take some grit and determination to get there. The cool thing is, the longer I practice new habits, the quieter the voice of fear becomes and the louder the voice of wisdom grows.

The Good

Realizing you're stuck is the first step to breaking yourself free.

The Bad

Doing things in a new way feels hard and awkward at first. It requires paying extra attention when we're making a new friendship: Am I drawn to this person because their dysfunction matches my dysfunction? Or am I drawn to them in a healthy way?

The Takeaway

1. Evaluate your past friendships that went south. Can you find a common thread? Why might that be?
2. Find your bearings. What kind of friendships do you want to make? What value is most important to you in your friendships?
   - Is it honesty?
   - Is it that they pursue you back?
   - Is it graciousness? That they're not easily offended?
   - Is it that they're a whole person? Not someone who is looking for you to save them?
3. Take a few minutes to think and jot down what matters to you. Just because you click doesn't mean they're the friend for you, because that click might be from years of dysfunction, not a sign to move forward.
4. Now map your way out. Figure out what habits you need to break, and what new habits you need to create to arrive at your desired destination.
5. Do it scared. Breaking cycles will bring up fear and insecurity—it just will. Old roles feel safe and known, new ones feel vulnerable.

It starts with you. We won't ever be able to change other people, but we can always change ourselves. Be the kind of friend you're longing for. Create healthy boundaries. Make steps toward healthy friendship.

CHAPTER 15

YOU'RE STUCK WITH ME LIKE POPCORN KERNELS IN YOUR TEETH

A Recipe for Healthy Attachment

"I don't want a whole dessert; let's just get two spoons."—Former friends of mine.
—Anna Kendrick

I (Jess) Velcroed my black light-up shoes after dumping out a pebble that had made its way up by my big toe. The shoes had gold stars on the side, and they were my greatest pride and joy. My mom had splurged on them at Walmart after I let her know that all light-up shoes were not created equal, and this exact pair was the pair of my dreams. I sat on the bench at the edge of the playground, and my friends Lacy and Tiffany walked by on their way to the slide.

"Hey!" I called out happily.

Lacy didn't respond and neither did Tiffany. They stared straight ahead and kept on walking.

I cleared my throat. "Hey guys!"

Lacy set her jaw, squinted her eyes, and purposefully kept her gaze on the slide. They kept on walking.

My stomach sank. I ran up behind them. "What's wrong?" Neither of them looked at me. "Can you please tell me?" I begged helplessly, an anxious knot forming in my gut.

Tiffany glared at me. "You know what you did."

"I don't. I don't know what I did," I said, the tears welling in my eyes.

"You told Trevor that Lacy likes him."

"What?" I said, confused. "I didn't—what do you mean?"

Lacy turned on me now. "I know you told him because *I can tell* that he knows, and who else would tell him?"

"What? I promise I didn't. Why do you think he knows?"

"*Because* I can just tell, and now I'm never going to be your friend ever again."

They stormed off and I ran to the bathroom before all of the third grade saw me break down in tears.

It was an awful day. I hung my head through lunch. I played alone in the afternoon. Finally, while I was drawing with chalk on the asphalt, Tiffany came over.

"Lacy is ready to speak to you," she said. She whipped around on her own pink Barbie light-up sneakers. They were so cool. I followed her to where Lacy was waiting beneath the monkey bars.

"I have decided to forgive you," she said. Relief washed over me. "*If...*"

My heart sank.

"*If* you admit you told Trevor."

"But I really didn't," I said.

"Then we're never going to be friends again," she sniffed. She wiped her hands on her jeans and started making her way across the bars like she didn't have a care in the world.

"Okay." I said.

"Say this," she commanded. "'I'M SORRY, LACY, THAT I TOLD TREVOR YOUR DEEPEST SECRET IN THE WHOLE WORLD.'"

The words felt wrong coming out of my mouth, but I felt I had no choice. I wasn't about to be friendless in the third grade. Besides, she was so angry I almost started to believe I had done what she said.

After I finished, she sniffed. "I'm still not ready to forgive you."

"But—"

Tiffany jumped in. "She said she's not ready."

"Ask me what you can do to make it up to me."

This was getting ridiculous, but I still felt I had no choice. "What can I do?"

"I want three days of your snack money," Lacy said unflinchingly.

I'd like to tell you that I said, "Sorry, that's not what friendship is about. I'm going to go hang out with some other kids." Or maybe, "I don't deserve to be treated this way, because I'm awesome, and I'm going to take my light-up star sneakers elsewhere."

But I didn't. I paid the girl.

⁓

Being alone has always been a fear of mine if I'm honest. I always figured I could do almost anything if I was with other people. This is probably why I had a gargantuan fear of being shipwrecked alone on an island, no matter that I'd never been on a ship before.

(Also, side note: Even though I saw it as a teen, *Cast Away* was traumatizing. Why that movie? Why did you do me that way, Tom Hanks?)

Sometimes when I make a friend, I sort of want them to sign a contract that they're not gonna leave or break my heart.

If I have a conflict with a friend and it feels unresolved, it's like my insides are turned inside out. I feel sick. I overthink it. I want to figure it out immediately and struggle with giving us both a moment to breathe. If there is conflict or disagreement, I deal with a lot of fear. Fear of losing them. Fear of being alone. Fear of the pain of disconnection.

I sometimes struggle to have boundaries because I don't want to let my friends down, and I want them to know I'm there. Plus I usually want to show up for them in whatever way possible. I tend to forget to look at my own capacity and needs and ask myself if it's good for me to say yes (even if I want to say yes). I tend to elevate my friends' needs over my own (and they didn't ask me to do that—it's my own deal). And if I'm brutally honest, I'm scared that if I don't make myself indispensable, they'll move on. I have to stay valuable (or so I think).

I hate being alone. Except after my kids go to bed at night and I get to watch my own shows and eat snacks. I call that my Netflix and Chill Spa. Alone with my own thoughts, though? I find myself exhausting. I am a lot. I am not always a joy to be with.

All of those things are a sign that I sometimes struggle with anxious attachment.

In the 1950s a psychoanalyst named John Bowby came up with the theory of attachment styles, and it was further developed by Mary Ainsworth. Attachment theory is based on the idea that our earliest relationships with caregivers set the stage for how we handle all kinds of relationships for the rest of our lives.[1]

A friend of mine first shared this with me, and it connected some missing pieces on how and why I do what I do in friendship. I hope it will for you too. It makes so much sense. *Of course* we all have a different foundation to start from when it comes to friendships.

As we dive in, here are a few important things to remember:

Your attachment style is not permanent (or it doesn't have to be). You may have been given a road map to connection that is full of holes and dysfunction, but learning where you began is the first step to filling in the missing pieces and starting a whole new story in your life.

You can't control other people and how they connect to you, but you can grow toward being healthy and whole in your ability to connect to them (and that's huge). This chapter will help you do that, as well as help you understand why some of your friends are the way they are. In a study done in 2020, 46 percent of participants were able to change their attachment style over two years.[2]

You can have more than one style of attachment, and that may change from relationship to relationship. For example, you might have secure attachment in your romantic relationships and an anxious attachment in your friendships. Or maybe one friendship feels secure and another triggers some avoidant attachment.

Attachment theory is based on our interaction with our care-givers; however, sources say we can be influenced by other relationships as well in our early years.[3] Maybe your parents were emotionally available, present, and consistent, but you were bullied or treated poorly by someone else. For me, it wasn't my parents. I think I was influenced primarily by moving around and losing core friendships. Everyone is different, so as you read, try not to box yourself in—it can look different for everyone.

Here are the four attachment styles:

Secure
Avoidant
Anxious
Disorganized[4]

We learn how to connect (or not) so young that some of it we can't even remember, but the good news is that if we learn what our styles are, it is totally possible to learn how to form secure attachments—a huge key in building long-term friendships.

Let's look at all four attachment styles and see what resonates with you.

SECURE

You might have secure attachment if the following are true:

- You felt secure with your caregivers from childhood and were able to ask for reassurance.
- You felt safe, comforted, understood, and valued as a kid. Your caregivers were likely emotionally available and emotionally self-aware.

If you have secure attachment, you have a leg up in your ability to connect with your friends. You're able to better regulate your emotions, trust your friends, communicate, be vulnerable about your emotions, self-reflect, handle conflict, and generally have a higher self-esteem. You also have an easier time setting and sticking to healthy boundaries.

In your friendships you are likely positive, trusting, and

loving. You believe you're worthy of belonging and you don't tend to struggle with a lot of jealousy.

AVOIDANT

You might have avoidant attachment if the following are true:

- You had emotionally distant or absent caregivers and felt rejection when you showed your emotional needs.
- You have felt on your own and that you couldn't depend on your caregivers. This could have been extreme neglect, or it could have been an overall busyness and preoccupation you sensed from them. They may have been overly focused on your performance in sports or your grades instead of your emotional needs.

If you have avoidant attachment you are likely to be highly independent and struggle to trust that you can rely on friends. You are also skeptical of people who want to be close to you. You likely hold your cards close and your friends at arm's length. You may bounce around in a lot of surface-level friendships but avoid growing truly close to anyone. Or you may find yourself thinking you don't really need anyone at all.

You may long for depth in your relationships but be unsure of why you can't seem to achieve it.

ANXIOUS

You might have anxious attachment if the following are true:

- You didn't know what to expect from your caregivers. Their interactions with you felt erratic and unpredictable, leaving you confused and unstable. They may have sometimes been very attuned to your needs and disconnected (or pushed you away) at other times.

- You may have felt responsible for how your caregivers felt.

If you have anxious attachment, you likely lean toward codependency and feel responsible for your friends' feelings. You may struggle with clinginess and what feels like an insatiable need for validation. You likely also have to deal with jealousy, being highly sensitive to criticism, and feelings of unworthiness in your friendships. It can seem very, very difficult to relax and trust.

You may long for security in yourself and your friendships but be unsure of why that desire feels impossible to achieve.

DISORGANIZED

You might have disorganized attachment if the following are true:

- You had a confusing and painful relationship with your caregivers, in which you experienced them as both your source of comfort and your source of fear.
- You experienced trauma in your childhood and specifically in the relationships that every child needs to be the safest. You saw your guardian as extremely inconsistent, unpredictable, and unreliable. While they may have been caring and nurturing in one moment, in the next they may have turned around and been neglectful, dismissive, or angry without reason. You never could trust what version of them you were going to get.

If you have disorganized attachment, you may feel confused as to what it is you want. It may feel like you want closeness, but at the exact same time you don't. You likely have behaviors from both avoidant and anxious attachment styles. You may have high levels of anxiety, fear, or rejection and difficulty regulating your emotions. You may feel desperate for connection and belonging in your friendships and also push your friends away. You probably believe that rejection is a guarantee, but you still seek connection (yet find yourself pushing away once you have it). You're desperate for connection and terrified of it at the same time.

Your friends may feel confused by what you want (and you may be confused too) but feel unsure of how to move forward.

Okay, that's a lot to process, but what attachment style sounds the most like you? Did any tug at your heart or whisper in your ear, "This one"? If you found yourself leaning toward avoidant, anxious, or disorganized, that's okay. You aren't alone and you are in fact a living, breathing, competent human who is capable of healing, growing, and changing. Here are a few practical tips to help you move toward a secure attachment in your friendships:[5]

Identify your attachment style. Hopefully one of these styles resonates with you and you feel seen. This isn't a test you pass or a commentary on how dysfunctional you may or may not be (we all are to some degree!)—it's just a starting point to healthier connection.

Consider therapy. Therapy is awesome. I love therapy! A trained professional is invaluable in reworking our attachment styles. I have been going regularly (whether I have a pressing struggle or not) for the last two years.

Seek friendships with people who have a secure(ish) attachment style. This will help you grow because we organically learn from the people we're closest to. We pick up on their traits. We absorb their general attitudes and we tend to adopt their ways of thinking. Make the decision to be influenced by people who have the qualities you're after.

Work on boundaries and assert your needs. I'm really working on this and it's hard. Caring for our friends and showing up for our friends are some of the most important building blocks of friendship. Having boundaries means I'm also caring for myself and showing up for myself. There's a fine line between intentionally pursuing and striving.

Practice grace and acceptance of yourself and your friends. You're not going to become secure overnight—it takes time and work. Be gentle, you're making the right steps. Yay! Go you! Start with grace for yourself. If you can practice being gentle with yourself, being gentle with others will come more naturally. None of us are perfect.

Slow down before you react. It takes work to stop doing what we've always done and responding how we've always responded. Slow down, recognize the triggers, and move yourself toward a healthier response. My counselor says this creates new pathways in my brain. Once we pack down that new pathway, it will be easier to go down it without as much work.

Work on self-soothing and self-nurturing. No friendship is ever going to be able to fill a void left by a deficit from childhood, and it's too much pressure. Practice self-compassion, take a bath, listen to music that heals your soul, or anything else that helps you relax.

I have parents who gave me a lot of the pieces required to build secure attachment, and the gift of that is not lost on me. Still, sometimes I'm secure, sometimes I'm avoidant, and I'm often anxious. In my own journey I'm working hard at boundaries in friendship and asking, *Am I being a good friend, or am I trying to earn friendship?* There's a big difference between the two. I'm working hard at not taking on other people's feelings. And I'm working hard at being okay if people are disappointed in me.

Listen, we're all just works in progress. There is no shame in the growth game. Will we always get it right? Heck no. But healing our own hearts and leaning into secure attachment will not only strengthen our friendships and get us past some roadblocks we've been feeling (and maybe couldn't put our finger on) but will also help us come into our own skin and breathe a sigh of relief. You are worthy. You matter.

I wish I could go back and give that little girl on the playground a hug. I wish I could tell her, "You're alright, and you don't ever have to earn friendship." I wish I could tell her, "Find someone else who looks lonely and play with them."

I can't go back, but I can keep growing and learning as a grown-up adult.

Let's grow there together.

The Good

Knowledge is power; it really is. I never even realized there was anything unique in the way I viewed friendship and relationships in general. It's so helpful to give my insecurities a voice and to know that even though this is where I started, it's not where I have to end.

The Bad

Chances are (unless you're a secure attachment all the way), you've sold yourself short in relationships in one way or another. Maybe you've withheld trust from people who really were safe. Maybe you've smothered a friendship by overdoing it out of fear.

The Takeaway

I feel like our first move here is self-compassion. Whatever the reason behind your attachment style, chances are there's some brokenness. Take a moment with me and look back at that little girl. Maybe she's bawling in the bathroom in her star light-up shoes. Maybe she feels alone in her own home. Maybe she's been the victim of abuse. Whatever your story, make sure you love yourself today. Now answer these questions:

1. What attachment style do you resonate with the most?
2. What work can you do to move toward security?

Remember as always, give yourself time and patience. Baby steps are the perfect size of steps.

CHAPTER 16

YOU ARE WELCOME IN MY HOME,
BUT MAYBE NOT IN MY BATHROOM

A Recipe for Boundaries

> Just a reminder that sometimes what you have to do
> is guard your own heart. And that's not an especially
> easy thing to do, but keep in mind that it's not about
> unforgiveness, unkindness, anger, or bitterness. It's
> about gently saying . . . his heart. It belongs to me,
> so I'll do whatever it takes to keep it pure, to keep it
> healthy, to protect and honor it.
> —Amy Weatherly

When I (Jess) walked into the gym and signed in at the front desk, I was suddenly excruciatingly aware of my leggings and the way they cut me in half like a bursting can of Pillsbury biscuits. Women filed past me through the open door. All of them looked like they modeled for *Fitness* magazine in their spare time.

Where are the normal people? Where are the ones with a stain on their shirt that they didn't see until right at this exact moment? I don't have my water. Shoot, how am I going to work out without water? I should pee. Do I have to pee? LORD, I DON'T EVEN KNOW IF I HAVE TO PEE.

I followed the women into the room, feeling like everyone could see my awkwardness like a flashing neon sign above my head. There weren't any spots at the back of the room. Shoot. The back of the room is where I thrive. Where should I even put my yoga mat? Does my yoga mat smell like sweat and like a girl who once fell over doing downward-facing dog? I hesitantly laid my mat between two people who—by some wizard-like sorcery at 6 a.m.— were wearing makeup. The instructor strode to the front of the room and we began.

Within five minutes sweat poured down my back. My legs screamed at me, my arms felt like they might give way. "TEN MORE!" she yelled above the music. *Ten more???* Well, this is it, I guess. This is where it all ends for me. Right here on this classroom floor with a stain on my shirt and professional athletes as my audience. Take me now, Jesus. I'm ready to go home.

Let's just all recognize that doing things for the first time is frightening. You can buy the right clothes and get the right water bottle, but nothing is going to adequately prepare you for doing the work except actually doing the work. This chapter might challenge some muscles you haven't used very often, but hang in there. Over time it gets easier.

I listened to a podcast of Brené Brown's recently, where she addresses believing that people are doing the best they can. She said, "All I know is that my life is better when I assume that people are doing their best. It keeps me out of judgment and lets me focus on what is, and not what should or could be."[1]

I'd heard that quote before, but somehow I'd missed an important part of it. I'd focused on the grace part, the not-judging part. Like I said in chapter 8, it was painful but good. I thought I "got" it. Overall it felt straightforward. Have compassion. Have grace. Realize that you have no idea what they've walked through or why they are where they are. It's hard, kinda like bench-pressing. Ouch, but I understand the assignment.

But it turns out I didn't fully get it at all.

In this podcast Brené goes on to talk about the second part that I'd never even fully registered: it "lets me focus on what *is*, and not what should or could be."[2]

The "what is."

Her sister, who is a therapist, said that when she helps people come around to believing others are doing the best they can, the most common reaction is *grief*.

When we actually believe that someone is doing the best they can, we accept what is. When I did this, the anger dissipated and the grief came in giant, crashing, spontaneous waves.

My guess is that it will for you too. The grief could look different for everyone.

They're not the friend we need them to be. That's real.

The story we saw playing out of our friendship was beautiful, and it ended ugly instead. That's devastating.

A person we love is not trustworthy, and we're going to have to implement boundaries to keep ourselves safe. That's painful.

A person we believed was for us and all-in on the friendship didn't value us or the relationship the same way we did. That's agonizing and can really mess with our emotions.

The disease of addiction has taken over their lives, and we

can't change it for them. We can't do the work on their behalf. That's such a heavy truth to swallow.

If I sit back and reevaluate the friendships where I've been hurt, and really boil them all down, I do genuinely believe they were doing the best they could. But it hurt like heck to accept that truth.

Anger and grace may be hard to hold in the same space, but grace and grief go hand in hand. Accepting things as they are means we are usually forced to let go of what we wanted them to be. It means we are forced into trading fantasy for reality, hypothesis for facts, and the pretty picture of how we imagined the friendship playing out for the messy events that have actually unfolded in real time.

This is where our own feelings, disappointments, and hurt land. They land in what *is*. We grieve in the *what is*, and it's also where we have to create boundaries.

I had married the "believing people are doing the best they can" part with the "believing they could magically do better" part. It felt like giving up on them somehow to not include the second part, but the reality was that I was keeping myself from accepting some hard truths. Being mad feels a lot simpler than grief. Being frustrated feels a lot simpler than grief. Overcommunicating, when communicating is clearly not working, is simpler than grief (for me), and defending myself and explaining my side of things over and over and over feels a lot simpler than grief. But refusing to accept what *is* kept me from drawing the boundaries I needed to implement for the sake of my own heart, and it kept me from grieving the things I needed to grieve.

It kept me from grieving over situations like this:

- A friend I really love who is not able to be a good friend to me right now, because they're doing the best they can.

- A friend who is an addict and doesn't want help. That's where they're at right now, as much as I wish they weren't. They're doing the best they can.
- A friend who is disappointed and negative, and they're going to stay disappointed and negative right now, because they're doing the best they can.
- A friend who continually lies and withholds pertinent information, while refusing to acknowledge how their dishonesty is hurtful right now, because they're doing the best they can.
- A friend who isn't able to have a vulnerable or real conversation with me right now, because they're doing the best they can.
- A friend who doesn't have the same vision for friendship, or the same capacity I have right now, because they're doing the best they can.
- A friend who isn't going to apologize to me in a way that is healing or helpful, because they're doing the best they can.

Now, after accepting where they actually are and then choosing to believe that they're doing the best they can, that they're giving what they're capable of giving, what do *I* need in these relationships? In a lot of them, if we have the history to support it, I'd first gently communicate. Things like, "Hey I'm worried about you," or "You've been in a really negative headspace lately and I'm wondering what's up," or "I'm checking on your heart because things seem off and I care about you." But I'm learning to recognize when it's not a communication issue and is actually a case where they're doing the best they can. Here are some examples:

For my friend who isn't able to be a good friend, and hasn't been able to be a good friend for a long time, I need to take some space and not invest so heavily. I need friendships that are mutual, so I'm going to need to pursue other people. I can't give enough for both of us. I have needs too.

For my friend who is an addict (and this one is more complicated), I need to grieve what addiction has done to them. I need to protect myself and my family from what that disease could do to me. I cannot get help for her—she has to decide to get help for herself. She isn't showing up for me right now because she isn't capable of it. She isn't thinking clearly right now because she isn't capable of it. She isn't being herself right now because she isn't capable of it. I love her, but this isn't a friendship.

Note: Addiction is not a character flaw. It's not a personality trait. It is an excruciating disease that is not simple or easy to fix, and just like I am not qualified to heal their broken leg, I am not qualified to heal their addiction.

For my friend who is disappointed and negative, I need to accept that their mindset is affecting me and that I don't feel filled with hope or joy or goodness when I'm around them right now. I need to limit my time with them so that I don't dry up my own reserves. I can spend some time with them, but not a lot of time.

For my friend who is chronically untruthful, I need to acknowledge that the trust between us has been damaged and that it isn't mine to repair. I cannot keep making excuses or patching up holes they are making. I need to watch what I say around them and be mindful of allowing what they say to me to be regarded as fact. I need to make sure I am not repeating any gossip they spread or having overly revealing conversations with them.

Trust is essential to every single relationship. I (Amy) always tell my kids that trust is like a bucket full of balls that connects me to them, and when they lie, one ball gets removed. At a certain point, after enough balls have been taken out of the bucket, our relationship gets difficult because I can't believe their words and take them at face value. None of us wants to admit it, but we all lie from time to time. Like most things, we have to look at the patterns and go from there. If someone has a pattern of lying, I have to admit that this is a relationship void and thus, it isn't a very safe or sturdy relationship.

For my friend who isn't able to do vulnerable or real conversation, I need to accept that I'm not going to be able to hash this all out *with* them. No amount of vulnerability and communicating on my part is going to bridge that gap. I have to accept that our relationship is surface level right now and get deeper connection elsewhere.

For my friend who has shown that they don't have the same vision on friendship, or don't have the same capacity for friendship I have, I need to take things for what they are and not let my mind go wild with expectations, or I will inevitably be disappointed. I can't expect them to have a deep friendship when they are looking for something more shallow. I can't expect them to give a lot of time or energy to the friendship when they don't have a lot of time or energy to give. If their investment is a small one, I have to accept that the friendship will likely be smaller as well, and that's okay. I can still enjoy their company. I can still look forward to being with them. I can still like them and appreciate their presence in my life, I just can't pile expectations on them that they are incapable or unwilling to meet. That's not fair for either of us.

For my friend who isn't able to apologize or help me find the closure I need, I have to accept that I'm going to need to find it outside my relationship with them. I'll need to work through it on my own and through therapy.

Accepting any and all of those realities leads me down a path to grief. I have to grieve that my friendship isn't what I expected it to be. I have to grieve that we can't walk through this season as closely as I thought we would. I have to grieve because they're suffering and hurting and there is nothing I can do to save them. As much as I may want to be their savior, I have to let Jesus stay in power. I'm only human. I have to grieve that this isn't how I pictured things going. I have to grieve that this isn't the way the story was supposed to be written. I have to accept that their heart belongs to them, and that my heart belongs to me and it is mine to guard.

Ugh. Right?

According to the University of Washington Counseling Center, there are five stages of grief:[3]

1. Denial
2. Anger
3. Bargaining
4. Depression
5. Acceptance

I have a theory that when we don't accept what *is*, it keeps us cemented in anger and denial and prevents us from moving through our grief. It keeps us from healing. It keeps us rooted in a broken place, and things have a hard time blooming when they are soiled in brokenness. When we establish boundaries, it's like we are creating little fences so we can allow the ground to bloom. The fences let us keep growing, but in a way that is both manageable and effective.

I had a nightmare about my broken friendship the other night. It's been years since things ended, but still those feelings bubble to the surface like a Diet Coke that's just been poured, and I know there is more work to do. I read somewhere that the cost of loving is oftentimes grief, and I feel that with every fiber of my being.

I wish I could package this all in a nice box. I wish I could give you the step-by-step plan that would keep it from being complicated or hard, but I can't. It is hard. It is messy. We have to learn as we go, or maybe a better way of putting it would be that we have to learn as we *grow*, because we are growing even when we don't feel like it.

I want you to know that whatever it is you are walking through, your feelings are normal. I want you to feel validated that grief in friendship is hard and painful, and there's no way to maneuver your way around the aches—there's only addressing them head-on.

And I want you to know that you are not alone.

You're working out muscles you likely have never worked before, and it's normal for it to feel impossible and awkward. Nobody walks up to a barbell for the first time and deadlifts three hundred pounds. You get there with small, feasible, do-able steps. (Or maybe you're like me and you perpetually use the two-pound weights and you're fine with that.) Boundaries are the same.

I heard something recently that kinda blew my mind. It was that the most compassionate people have good boundaries.[4] Meaning they say no, they take care of themselves, and they're honest about what they can and can't do. They value their own needs and health.

I think it feels so backward to us (especially people pleasers) because deep down we believe bending over backward and growing bitter and burnt-out is "the right thing." We think in order to be "good people" we can't say no. In reality we're pouring ourselves out until there's nothing left to pour, and our true compassion is completely dried up like a raisin. I'm no sommelier, but I don't think you can make wine from raisins. You need the plump, juicy fullness of a grape.

The other day I walked into another exercise class. I still don't do them very often, but a friend of mine had invited me and I thought I'd give it a try. Memories of other classes like the one at the beginning of this chapter haunted me as I walked through that door, once again surrounded by people who definitely seemed like they knew what they were doing.

Except this time I'd been practicing at home. Nothing crazy, mind you. Fifteen minutes here, thirty minutes there. I found it helped my peace levels to have a physical outlet, and home videos were perfect for me (although they gave me major flashbacks of my mom in the '80s working out to Jane Fonda). I still felt nervous finding a space to squeeze in my mat among all the others, and I still wondered if I should pee one more time before class began. But this time, when the instructor strode to the front and began to call out instructions, I noticed I felt more confident. When she called "TEN MORE!" I was shocked to realize I could do it. It wasn't easy, but I also didn't feel like I was going to press my Life Alert button while collapsing on the floor.

Boundaries are like that too. It feels hard to say no. It feels scary. It feels like showing up to gym class for the very first time. But the more you do it, the easier it will become. The game changed for me when I realized that boundaries weren't about pushing people away, locking them out, or unkindness. They are about preserving the relationships in a way that makes sense, keeps things healthy for both parties, and creates a safe environment.

Yes, sometimes this means I have to grieve a little. Since my entire life flows from my heart, I have to protect it. The dream I had of a perfect friendship, where we endlessly give to each other with no consequences, has to give way to reality. I need to protect my heart. Setting boundaries means that I have to acknowledge my own needs and accept that I can't expect people to give and do more than they are capable of. It means that I refuse to lose myself in the pursuit of any friendship. I've done it before. Zero out of five stars. Do not recommend.

The Good

The more you're able to accept what is, to have grace, and to make boundaries accordingly, the healthier you'll become. It's hard work, but it's absolutely worth it.

The Bad

Grief hurts. It sounds cliché, but it's true. I don't think we talk enough about the grief of losing friends (or friendships changing). I did some googling about how long it takes to get over a friendship breakup and I came up pretty empty-handed. A few months was a suggested time span, but that has not been my experience. Maybe for short friendships, but not for long ones. Out of curiosity I started googling how long it takes to get over long dating relationships or even divorce. Although it's not the same, close friends are deeply intertwined in your life in intimate ways. Breakups aren't simple or easy. The results I got resonated with me. Some experts say it takes an average of two years to heal from a long-term dating relationship or divorce, while others say it can take as long as half the years you were together. I firmly believe the same holds true for long-term friendships.

The Takeaway

Think specifically about the friendships you're struggling in and answer these questions:

1. Are you relating to these friends as they are or as you believe they could be?
2. Is your love for them, and your vision of the person you think they're capable of being, blinding you to the reality of who they are right now?
3. If they're doing the best they can and you accept the reality of what is, what boundaries do you need to put in place to protect who you are?

I know it's hard, but have courage. You can do this.

CHAPTER 17

I KNOW YOU LIVE 1,200 MILES AWAY, BUT CAN YOU BE HERE IN FIVE MINUTES?

A Recipe for Doing Long-Distance Friendship

> There is magic in long-distance friendships. They let you relate to other human beings in a way that goes beyond being physically together and is often more profound.
> —attributed to Diana Cortes

My (Jess's) goal is always to be intentional about who I'm investing my friend-energy into. I have kids, so I'm basically an unpaid and unappreciated Uber driver. I'm also a personal chef and professional snack-getter for said kids. I'm a wife. I'm an author and blogger, and my laundry pile is like the curse that keeps on cursing. These people refuse to stop wearing clothes.

Sadly, I have only so much friend-energy to give. My cup runneth on near-empty when it comes to stamina. I wish I had endless capacity. I wish I didn't need alone time to recharge. I wish I didn't need at least eight hours of sleep, but I do. I'm actually a big fan of that sleep. Sometimes I get so excited about an early bedtime that I can't actually fall asleep. It's a real issue.

After my family (aka the time-suckers), I have time to prioritize only a handful of relationships. We always have the choice between investing a large amount of time into a small number of friends and going deeper with those relationships, or investing a small amount of time into a larger number of friends and staying more surface-y. I choose to go the fewer-friends route. Belonging over popularity every single time.

Most of my friends live within a ten-mile radius and that is nice. In fact, I regularly encourage my in-town friends to move even closer to me. I want them in my neighborhood. I want them down my street. I want regular backyard barbecues, and I want to walk barefoot to their house and let myself in the front door after a long day. I want to raid their fridge. I want our families to have water-gun fights in the summer. I want a little cul-de-sac made up entirely of my people. This is the dream, and you'd better believe I am constantly sending these friends information on houses that go for sale near me, as though moving houses is quick and easy and no big deal and mortgage rates aren't ridiculous.

And then there's the one friend who lives approximately 1,269.7 miles away. Her name is Amy, and the fact that she lives halfway across the country is dumb, but we are truly like-hearted. We are each other's people, and we knew it from the moment Amy slid into my DMs.

Amy is Texan, and when I say Texan, she is *Tex-an*. I have never heard of having a state anthem or drive-thru shops that just sell sweet tea. I have lived in a lot of places and I have very little state loyalty. She was deeply disappointed—nay, offended—when she found out I had worked at a Dairy Queen in Montana, because she said there is an actual Dairy Queen song in Texas that says Dairy Queen is only in Texas. That is the most Texas thing I've ever heard. Listen, Texas, let us have Blizzards, too, 'kay? Amy has given me the gift of ranch water as well as an appreciation for squeezing lime and a dash of salt directly onto a tortilla chip (if you haven't done that yet, I give it five stars—highly recommend).

Amy is the actual queen of shoes. She loves shoes, and although she has rubbed off on me, I recently realized that the only time I buy new shoes is when I am with her. We have stuff in common, but we also have a whole lot that's different.

But she is undoubtedly and unequivocally my people.

Okay, my (Amy's) turn here. Jess is a Northern Californian / Montanan / World Traveler / Southern Californian. Her hometown identity is confused, and her roots grow out of a lot of different places. Coffee is the vehicle on which her personality drives. No coffee, no personality. That's just the way it is.

Jess is a snack person. She is never going to go to a place where there is not a snack. She rewards herself with snacks. Went grocery shopping? Congrats! You now have a snack from the checkout line. She does a chore—snack. She can't handle any sort of meeting without snacks because that is actual torture. While I sing everywhere I go, Jess will break into spontaneous dancing wherever she is. She's not a professional dancer, but she makes up for that with passion and ridiculousness.

Jess is queen of the throw pillow. How many throw pillows are too many? This is a question her husband, Graham, asks, but the answer is obvious. NO NUMBER OF THROW PILLOWS IS

TOO MANY. Jess does not clean her face. I wear a Darth Vader mask to bed, which looks slightly demonic, but Jess is getting used to it after a few girls' trips.

We are different. (Not about the throw pillows, though, obviously.)

Like I said before, we have stuff in common, but we also have a whole lot that's different. If Amy were a painting, there would be a lot of neon and sparkles. There would be blues and yellows and pinks. If I (Jess) were a painting, there would be a lot of neutral, but hopefully still some sparkle. I'd be the painting equivalent of bedazzled Birkenstocks.

But we are 100 percent each other's people, and we have learned how to make our long-distance friendship not just work but flourish. Our friendship has become even more essential as we've navigated difficult seasons of loss. We've leaned heavily on each other for supper, advice, and encouragement.

Sometimes Amy calls and I let it go to voicemail. Not because I'm ignoring her but because I'm hastily tossing shoes and socks and old fast-food paper bags over the backseat so the kids will have room to sit when I pick them up from school.

I'll get a text: Jess, pick up. I need to see you.

One sec. I text back.

I put my car in Park and FaceTime her. I hope and pray everything is okay in her world. I prepare for the worst. Anxiety is filling up the inside of my chest. I can feel my heart beating faster and faster. Amy answers on the first ring with a huge grin on her face. She's trying to hold back her smile and act chill. She's failing. My anxiety dies and excitement takes over.

"I need to know something," she says. "Do you like my shirt?"

I squint at the Hawaiian-style button-up she's wearing. It's definitely out of the norm from the loungewear and graphic tees she normally sports. I notice something printed all over it.

"OH MY GOSH. IS THAT MY FACE?!"

She bursts into giddy laughter and leans back in her chair so I can fully take in the glory and hilarity of seeing someone wear a shirt with my face all over it. I'm not exactly the Rolling Stones, so this is a first for me.

"I missed you." She shrugs.

I don't know what the other parents thought was happening in my car as I burst into hysterical laughter, but I can guarantee it wasn't that.

"Don't worry, I sent you some socks with my face on them just in case you're missing me too," she cracks up, rightfully proud of her shenanigans.

———

Amy is living proof that you can be a really good friend even when you live one bajillion miles away (and we do live one bajillion miles away from each other).

I've seen her dance in her front yard in a fully inflatable costume while her kids held the phone to FaceTime someone happy birthday. She is the queen of ordering cookies and sending gifts. She uses her precious spare minutes to call you. She makes you feel important, like you matter, like she's happy to have you in her life, and that's a gift you can give no matter what the distance between you may be.

She and I basically have a constant stream of texts and voice memos going. She laughs at the way I send forty-five separate texts to say one complete thought. I love how she tells me not to talk for a minute when she opens her car doors so the kids can climb in after school (so the teachers don't judge her for being on the phone during car line).

The thing about long distance is you just really don't have time for anything other than real. You've gotta just get down to it. It's like the difference between a four-hour movie and a thirty-minute short film. A short film is going to cut out the nonsense and the fluff. There's no time for it.

"Hey, today is the worst and everyone hates me."

"Good morning, I'm thinking we should run away and take a vacation to Tahiti . . . tomorrow. I'm looking up flights."

"Fighting with the husband currently. Also I'm going to the bathroom right now so just ignore the flush?"

"Currently at HomeGoods about to buy a plant I don't need."

"Sigh. I'm really struggling. I feel a wave of depression coming on. I know I'll make it through, but it's tough right now. Can you say a prayer for me?"

Every good and lasting friendship requires intentionality, whether they live next door or on another planet. And when you're intentional in your friendships, it means you do them with purpose and on purpose. It means you plan accordingly and you don't take them lightly. It means you care enough to focus on them—like a plant you really want to survive—so you water them and tend to them regularly.

Some friendships can withstand distance. Some cannot, and that's okay, but it's important to recognize and to continue to feed into the friendships that are capable of withstanding some empty miles of space. Living far away is not an immediate deal-breaker. It does mean you probably need to find a different emergency contact and a different errand buddy. It's pretty hard to call up someone who lives hundreds or even thousands of miles away and say, "Hey, I need someone to drive me home from my colonoscopy at 2 p.m. Can you be here?"

The friendship between Amy and me is precious, and the only thing I hate is that I can't just walk in her front door and plop on her couch whenever I feel like it. I want to raid her closet. I want to hang out in the backyard where she spends so much of her time. I want to cheer on her kid who plays soccer, but I love that she's never more than a phone call away.

⌇

Over the last couple of years, we've figured out a few tips and tricks for making long-distance friendships work. Here are some of our favorites:

Get good at keeping it short and sweet. I don't know about you, but one of the things that has kept me away from phone calls is that I don't generally have the time for a one- or two-hour convo (even if I'd like to). If there were a magic potion for creating more hours in a day, I'd share it with you. But there isn't. Twenty-four hours is what we have. It's all we'll ever have, so Amy and I have gotten really, really skilled at talking for the few precious minutes we have and then saying "kloveyoubye" or "kidsarefightingcallyoulater."

We even have a mutual understanding that if we have something happen while we're on the phone that must be dealt with immediately (such as a kid is hurt, the principal walks up during school pickup for a chat, or we just dropped a bottle of olive oil and broke it all over the grocery store floor), we just hang up and call back later. If you are going to have long-distance friendships, or deep friendships for that matter, things cannot be fragile. Nobody can walk on eggshells.

You can and should think about the other person's feelings, but you cannot live by their feelings. You can't fret and stress about each and every tiny move. It's too exhausting. You have to establish a mutual trust that you are both doing the best you can, and you're never hurting the other person maliciously or purposely. Hanging up without a word is a really crummy thing to do with someone you barely know, or with someone you're in the process of building a relationship with, but once it's been established . . . sometimes you've gotta do what you've gotta do. Short, brief, to the point, regular catch-ups are a must.

Take advantage of the fact that you don't live in the same town or know all of the same people. Long-distance friends are a vault in which you can deposit all your vent sessions and unfiltered frustrations. "Someone hurt my feelings and I don't know what to do. I'm furious at this friend, and I'm not sure how to handle my frustrations." This situation happened, and I need someone on the outside to look at it and give me a clear and honest perspective. I'm feeling all the things, and I need a safe space to verbally process without feeling like I'm gossiping or spreading rumors.

When you're in a long-distance friendship, your friend probably doesn't even know the other person. Your secrets are going nowhere. They're not going to judge the other person or feel awkward when they run into them at the Target checkout. She's the perfect person to offer unbiased advice and a listening ear.

Learn each other's preferred method of communication. Amy loves calls. I love long-winded text conversations and ridiculous voice memos that include off-key singing. We do them all. We both compromise. We both bend a little, because connecting with each other is more important than *how* we connect with each other. So if Amy wants to call, I'm down, even if it's not my preferred method. And if I want to send seven voice memos in a row, I send them, knowing Amy will respond even though it's not her favorite method. We love each other too much to be unwilling to bend. Some ways to keep in touch include

- phone calls,
- texting,
- voice memos,
- FaceTime,
- Marco Polo,
- walkie-talkie apps,
- sending cookies or flowers,
- sending funny videos,
- tagging each other on Instagram,
- watching a TV show separately then discussing it later,
- making a playlist you think they'd like, and
- having Grubhub deliver their favorite meal when they've had a hard day.

Ask, What can you handle today? This one is major because we can't read each other's faces unless we're FaceTiming. (We rarely are since we're both occupied with trying to reach the bottom of that cursed laundry pile. Where are all these underwear coming from?!) We both have a ton going on in our lives, and sometimes we're emotionally tapped out. If we want to talk through something heavy, first we'll ask, "What can you handle today?" before dumping our problems on the other person. If it's not a high-capacity day, we'll keep things light. If we have room mentally for the exchange, we'll let the other one lay it all on us. Amy thought of this during 2020, and it's been a healthy practice of ours ever since.

Maximize your time IRL. I hate that I can't see Amy all the time, but she is a fabulous travel buddy. When we're together, we have our own little traditions. We research the best brunch spots and eat until we hurt. We shop (probably at Nordstrom Rack) and try on ridiculous sunglasses for each other while acting like children in the shoe aisle. We find hole-in-the-wall Mexican food and eat again. We talk nonstop, and we watch TV with bags full of either Trader Joe's snacks or stuff we bought at the local gas station. Sometimes Amy has cookies delivered late at night. We have never once cared about staying at a fancy resort or touring a cool city. It's all about togetherness, so the destination matters little. It's all about finding a time that works for both of us and getting some cheap flights.

Ask thoughtful questions. You aren't likely to naturally know what's going on in your friend's day-to-day life. You won't know what errands they ran or whether their kid is sick. You won't know whether they stayed in and did laundry or went to a coffee shop and worked. You won't know what they ordered from the coffee shop or what they were wearing, so you're going to have to learn to ask questions. Find out what's going on in their world so you can feel more a part of it.

Remind each other regularly of how much you value the friendship. We send each other cookies or buy each other flowers. Things that say, "Hey, you over there 1,200 miles away, I'm thinking of you right now and even if we aren't together-in-city, we're together-in-heart."

I do not embellish when I say that Amy and I have walked through some of our coldest, harshest, and roughest seasons together since first becoming friends, and we have been there for each other in a real and tangible way.

Amy is not replaceable in my life. Her vibrancy, her voice, and her sparkle enrich my life. She enriches my whole life. Yeah, it would be nice to make spontaneous plans to meet up on a Tuesday night, but I've learned to love our long-distance friendship for exactly what it is. You lose some things, but you gain some things too. You give some, but you take even more.

Amy here. Compliments make me so uncomfortable, and Jess bragged on me way too much, so let me take a second to sing her praises.

Jess has carried me through more crap than just about anyone else. She has been there and she has stood by me. She has been understanding. There have been times when she has done 90 percent of the work to make this friendship last, and she has done it without putting pressure on me or making me feel guilty.

She is maybe the easiest person in the world to be around. I've never seen her judge another human. I've never seen her puff herself up. She is humble and down-to-earth to her core. I feel lighter when we're together, and my heart is always happy just knowing that she's in my corner. She has randomly sent me voice memos where she is praying for me, and she recently had a Mrs. Fields cookie cake delivered to my house with an encouraging and hilarious message on it. I wish I could share the message here, but I can't. That one stays in our friendship only! She never forgets what's going on with my kids. I hold on to her with a fairly tight grip, because I could never imagine my life without her.

And that's the only way long-distance friendships survive. They survive with intentionality. They survive with effort. They survive with creativity and gratitude and love, and I think most of all, they survive because we make a conscious decision that they are a plant worth watering. When you have been blessed enough to find a like-hearted friend in this crazy world, you have to go for it. You have to play all your cards and you have to figure it out, because even if they live a couple thousand miles away, you know your soul has a home in theirs.

The Good

Looking beyond our front yards opens a world of possibilities to friendship. We can find people who truly are cut from the same cloth. In this day and age we're no longer limited by who we see at the grocery store. We can call. We can FaceTime. We can fly across the country to meet each other.

The Bad

There are hard things about long-distance friendship. It takes a little extra work to maintain. Dang it, we wish we could just Star-Trek ourselves to their front steps whenever we feel like it.

The Takeaway

Don't undervalue friends who live far away. Take a minute to ask yourself who is highlighted as a friend in your life. If you haven't considered friends who don't live close, open your mind a little bit. Who are you supposed to invest in during this season?

If someone comes to mind who is long distance, text them and tell them how much they matter to you and make a plan to connect on a call.

CHAPTER 18

I'M TOO OLD TO SUCK IN MY BELLY, SO MY JEANS WON'T BUTTON

A Recipe for Knowing When to Walk Away

I am not pregnant, but I've had three kids and there is a bump. From now on, ladies, I will have a bump and it will be my baby bump. It's not going anywhere.

—Jennifer Garner

I (Jess) have always loved to win people over. At my first job, one of the regulars was an elderly man who was grumpy and snapped at us every time he came in. We weren't fast enough, his burger had too much ketchup, we forgot he wanted napkins. There was always something and no one could stand him. I announced that I was going to make him smile, and it was my summer-long challenge. I went out of my way to be extra kind. I went above and beyond to make his experience the very best. I talked to him about things he was interested in, like fishing (I like fishing about as much as I like cleaning toilets). He continued to go above and beyond to be the absolute worst. But one hot July day it happened. His salt-and-pepper mustache turned up at the corners when he saw me coming and he gave me a friendly greeting. He took his cheeseburger without complaint, and from then on he was friendly and I was his favorite. For years he lit up when I saw him around town.

———

There's a certain magic to winning people over. There's something special about making someone feel like they are the only one in the room when you're with them. It's a gift to make someone feel truly seen and heard.

I don't think we're supposed to win over our friends though. Maybe at first, but not long term. We can win over coworkers. We can win over the baristas at our favorite coffee shop. We can win over in-laws, our kids' friends, and that neighbor that gives us the evil eye when we roll into the driveway a little too fast. But friends shouldn't be won over, strived for, or chased after. They should like us for who we are, and we should like them for who they are too.

In friendship we should both be seen for who we are—not for what we do, not for our opinions, not for what we own, not for the way we make someone feel. We should both be appreciated. We should both be wanted. It doesn't work if any of this goes in only one direction. It doesn't work if we see them but hide ourselves. I learned that recently, and I learned it the hard way.

I didn't even know I was trying to win over my friend, but our relationship had turned into me striving to be who she wanted me to be. I knew it bothered her when I did certain things, so I stopped. I knew it annoyed her that I had specific quirks, so I worked hard to be less that way. I knew she judged the napkins and the empty water bottles on the floor of my car, so I rushed to clear them out of the way whenever she rode with me. I knew I wasn't exactly the friend she wanted me to be, so I tried to become the friend she wanted. I knew she didn't appreciate that I had a tendency to talk a lot, so I tried to take a backseat. I had less opinions, less excitement to share, and I always pivoted to whatever she wanted to do.

And the crazy thing is (or maybe not crazy at all), it wasn't enough. My efforts were never going to be enough. No matter how much I gave or how much I did, it was never going to meet her expectations. I was always destined to be both too much and not enough in her eyes, so the friendship fell apart. It hurt at first. Sometimes it still does if I let myself think about it for too long, but in a way, I see the beauty in that breakup too. I may have lost her, but I found my way back to me.

I shouldn't have been trying to win over one of my closest friends. I shouldn't have had to try so hard. There's making an effort and there's making too much effort. Maturity is knowing the difference. I should have been paying attention to the warning signs that the relationship between us wasn't working. What her critiques were really saying were, *You're not my person anymore. I don't enjoy you anymore.* But instead of reading the writing on the wall, I went into overdrive trying to be who she wanted me to be, and let's be honest, I probably did it terribly because at the end of the day, I am who I am.

We have to recognize the difference between constructive feedback and "I don't like you." Iron sharpens iron. It does. When my closest friends say, "Hey, I think you're missing it here," I listen. If they say, "When you said this, it hurt my feelings," I apologize

and make it right. But if everything I do and say is regularly causing offense, that's different.

The truth is, that particular friend wasn't my type of person
either—not really. I'm pretty laid-back and I like a lot of different
people, but when we were together it started to feel like when you
try to connect two positive energy magnets. It's just impossible
and they push up against each other. I hid more and more of who
I was, and she probably did too. I feigned interest in things I'm not
interested in. I held myself in, squeezed myself tight, bent over
backward like I was trying to make it under a limbo bar. It became
more like a job than a friendship. There just wasn't any breathing room.

I want to be around people who want to be around me. I'm too old
for negative energy and life is hard enough as is, so I hope that positive energy flows between us and I hope it flows well. I've come
too far and I've wasted too much time in the past to waste time in
the present.

I also understand that I'm not for everybody. As much as I try,
I know I'm draining to some and in spite of my best efforts and
your best efforts, sometimes the connection just isn't there. You
can't be everyone's favorite, ya know? To some, I'm the sand that
helps them build a castle, and to others I'm the sand that rubs them
the wrong way. I haven't always understood this, but I get it now.

I think one of the wisest things we can possibly do is own
who we are. We're meant to grow, we're meant to mature, but
we're not meant to be someone other than who we already are.
Sometimes we go through a heavy pruning to be the healthiest
version of ourselves. We're like a fruit tree in the wintertime—it

can be a little scary when we see those giant clippers, but a snip here and a snip there will only help us grow more into who we're supposed to be. It will help us be healthier and bear more good fruit. I'll tell you what pruning is not, though: pruning is not chopping at the trunk and hoping it becomes a different tree entirely.

Real talk: Sometimes you need to ask yourself if it's something you need to change about you, or if it's the friendship that needs to change. And sometimes it's the friendship that needs the snip.

You can be the healthiest tree imaginable, but if you're an apple tree, you're going to make apples. If someone is looking for oranges, they need to move on to a different tree instead of demanding that you produce what they want.

Our job is to become the best apple tree we possibly can. It's not to satisfy people who don't like apples.

Say you're a talker and a friend says, "Hey, sometimes you interrupt me when I'm talking, and it drives me nuts." That's something you can work on and grow in. I'm an interrupter and I'm constantly working to not do that, because it is hurtful and rude—especially with my quieter and more introverted friends. That's healthy, that's pruning.

If you're a talker and a friend lets you know they think you talk too much and they wish you were quieter, or if they feel like you have too many opinions and too much to say—spoiler, you're not their people. If they roll their eyes every time you're loud or you get animated when telling a story, that's not about you. That's about them wanting oranges instead of apples. That's not pruning, that's hacking at the trunk.

If you're an opinionated person and a friend says, "Hey, sometimes I don't feel like you listen or value my opinions when I share them because you're so convinced of your own, and honestly it makes me feel kinda stupid," that's something you can work on. Keep your opinions, but work on valuing the ones around you too.

Work on communicating in a way that doesn't make your friend feel stupid.

If you're an opinionated person and your friend wants you to stop being opinionated, that's not going to work. That's the way you're wired, the way you're made, and what they need isn't for you to change. What they need is to get over it or find a more passive friend.

Does that make sense?

Growth is good, but becoming someone else for the sake of a friendship isn't good at all. We want to surround ourselves with friends who will run with us toward the things in our hearts. We want to surround ourselves with friends who champion us becoming the very best version of ourselves. We want to surround ourselves with friends that like us. We want to surround ourselves with friends that love us even when we're a giant mess.

Sometimes people act like the only two options are being best friends or being mortal enemies, and I don't subscribe to that notion in the least. There are plenty of gray areas and there are plenty of relationships that fall in between those two extremes. It's okay if that's where some of us land.

I hope no one feels forced to hang out with me. I hope no one feels obligated to have lunch, or coffee, or even engage in a phone call with me. Everyone is off the hook—no ill will, no bitterness, no awkwardness. I still love them and want good for them. We will always be friendly, kind, and polite when we run into each other.

Time is short and everyone deserves to spend what they have with people who add genuine value, who bring life to their soul, who are peaceful for their heart. If I'm not that for someone, it's okay. My ego can handle it. I'm in a place where I want to be around people who want to be around me.

I hope if I say the wrong thing once, people will give me grace, and I hope they'll forgive me if I have a hard season where I kind of suck. Nobody will ever be perfect, so please don't hold me to that standard, but overall, if the person I am is not the person they need—let me go.

We both need the freedom to find genuine, deep friendship—the kind that helps us breathe easier and walk through life a little straighter—that nudges you forward and then holds you back when you're walking toward the edge of a huge mistake.

Life's just too short for the fake stuff. It's too short for pretending and walking on eggshells. The truth is, the thing one person hates about me may be what another person loves. Let's stop wasting time trying to change who we are when *who we are* is the gift we give to the world.

Up until recently, I'd let go of only one friendship in my entire life, and even that wasn't what I'd call a good, solid, close friendship. (It was an acquaintance and I didn't have much of a choice when it came to walking away because it was extremely toxic and a situation where I was clearly being taken advantage of, so it only barely counts.) I'm talking about every friendship I've ever had, going all the way back to kindergarten.

I will stay. Almost no matter what, I will stay.

This has always been a badge of honor I've worn with self-righteousness, almost a holier-than-thou sense of pride.

Look at me, everyone. I'm so good and virtuous and loyal that I have never ended a friendship. It has always been the other person's fault. I am without blame. I get friendship-dumped a lot, but that's not the point. The point is . . . I am pure. Wow. Gold medal, highest podium, blue ribbon for me.

I think I've always had an inclination to be a little self-righteous. I didn't mean to, and I definitely didn't think I was better than anyone else. I was just raised in a super conservative home where a super conservative church was our family fortress, and I was terrified to make a mistake. Any mistake. I was terrified to hurt anyone.

I was terrified to have anything less than a five-star reputation. I was terrified to . . . I was just terrified of a lot of things.

The truth is, there are no gold medals for holding on to friendships that have clearly run their course. There is no award for staying in places where you don't need to be. Maturity is facing the harsh truth that sometimes the season you're in needs to be a season of release.

Something I've been working on lately is understanding that the ultimate goal of friendship isn't for it to last forever. Forever is nice, but it isn't always doable. This doesn't need to be some fairy-tale thing. This is real life where messes exist and things get real.

A friendship that has ended isn't necessarily a friendship that has failed. The goal of friendship, I think, is to be a relationship that is full of love. A relationship where both people feel safe and come alive. A relationship where both people value each other and feel comfortable being themselves—on their best days and on their worst days.

And so I've taken the pressure of *forever* off my friendships. I hope they do go the distance, but I've learned to put my focus on the present day more than what may or may not happen in the future. Is the relationship healthy right now? Is it full of goodness at this moment? If it's not, are there things I can do to get it back on track? Is the stain on our friendship made of dirt, or is it made of bacon grease?

Accepting things for what they are can be so hard. We want to be in charge. We want to be able to patch things up and slap a Band-Aid on and pretend it's all fine, but some things just don't mend and some wounds just don't heal.

Sometimes the only thing to do is appreciate it for what it was, but open up the cage and let it out into the wild so it can be what it really needs to be.

We are meant to be who we are.

The right people will love it.

I want you to find your people.

And I want to find mine.

It's okay if some of us aren't that for each other. No love lost, only new friendships to be found for all of us.

Friendship isn't the place to suck in our bellies and force ourselves into boxes we don't fit in. Friendship is the place for the realest of reals, both for yours and for theirs. Friendship is the place to experience belonging, and as long as we are pretending to be someone we're not, we'll never truly belong. Even if we can convince other people to buy into our acting, we'll know. Even if we can convince them that this little show is enough, we'll know. We can run from loneliness. We can run from other people. But we can't ever run from ourselves.

Living with the goal of winning over our friends really isn't living at all. Now when we learn to relax and to be ourselves—that's when we win. That's when we all win.

The Good

You don't need to change who you are. You are wonderful exactly as you are. Do you talk a lot? Awesome. Are you quiet? Awesome. Are you creative and artistic? Awesome. Are you a thinker and a natural analyst? Awesome.

The Bad

Being honest with ourselves can be painful. It's particularly hard when you have a lot of history in a friendship. The thing is, sentimentality isn't a reason to hang on to it. It feels like it is, but it's not.

The Takeaway

Evaluate your friendships. Are those people helping you grow or are they wishing you would change into a different person entirely? Just like a marriage, it's not good to choose someone while thinking they'll become who you want them to be. We are who we are.

If you realize you're in a friendship with someone who'd love to cut you down right at the roots, what do you do? The good news is that it doesn't have to be a big, dramatic breakup—it can just look like starting to invest your friend-energy into other people. It can be making peace with growing apart.

If you realize you're in a friendship with someone and you would like to cut them down right at the roots, what do you do? Stop trying to change them. Stop trying to make the friendship into something it's not. What you need is a different friend, not for this person to change who they are. Apple trees are going to make apples.

CHAPTER 19

WE SHARE A FENCE, BUT I DON'T EVEN KNOW YOUR NAME

A Recipe for Knowing Your Neighbors

A friend may be waiting behind a stranger's face.
—Maya Angelou

I (Amy) didn't really know our neighbors for the first five years we lived in our old house. They lived right there and we had spoken maybe twice. It was one of those situations where I should have known their names. We'd introduced ourselves at some point, so I'd look like a jerk if I asked now. But I still didn't know their names, so I had to toss out a general "Howdy, neighbor! Hey youuu!" when I'd see them. I don't know what this says about me, but I did know their dog's name.

We didn't have any issues, but we didn't have any connection either. I chalked it up to there not being any click between us personality-wise and eventually stopped making any effort whatsoever. If I needed eggs in a pinch, oh well. I'd just run to the grocery store or figure something else out. Every once in a while, we'd pass each other going in and out of houses, but we mostly ignored each other.

Then the pandemic hit. We were all outside all the time. We were kind of forced into a relationship, and that turned out to be such an unexpected blessing.

My neighbor's name was Jennifer and we became close. We'd sit outside and chat. Her kids would come outside to play with the water hose with my kids. My daughter would run over and play Barbies with her daughters. I'd give her hand-me-down clothes and she'd let me borrow sugar for chocolate chip cookies.

And then—as if everything wasn't already hard enough in the pandemic—Jennifer learned she had breast cancer. She was young. She was healthy. And still . . . cancer. She was going to need a handful of surgeries as well as chemo. It was a road full of gravel and speed bumps and the unknown.

During those rocky months, Jennifer invited me into her real. She invited me into her mess, into her tender places and fragile spaces. She needed my help, but I'm the one who left with the gift.

After one particular surgery where she couldn't lift her right arm or get her chest wet, Jennifer asked me if I would come over and wash her hair in the sink for her. It was the most intimate, almost holy experience—to be invited into someone's sacred space. Something like that will bond you real fast.

We've moved to a new neighborhood across town since then, but the lesson of knowing the people who live near remained with me. So from the day we moved in, that became my mission—to not let five years pass before meeting my neighbors. We didn't have to be best friends, but I hoped to form some kind of relationship.

So far, things have gone pretty well. In fact, three of the neighborhood kids are over playing as I'm writing this chapter. They walk back and forth between our two houses, and it's been a godsend. They know where I keep the popsicles and they feel comfortable enough to help themselves. They play football in the front yard and they make up games using hockey sticks and wiffle balls. Sometimes they fight, but after a day or two, all is forgotten and everybody is back playing.

There's a family with younger kids directly across the street, and that's been a special gift as well. My eleven-year-old son will shoot basketball hoops with their six-year-old son. It's given my son the ability to learn how to be patient and giving and kind with someone younger than him.

I have a neighbor-turned-friend who will randomly drop off a twelve-pack of Diet Dr. Pepper on my front porch. I have another neighbor whose son took care of our animals while we were out of town during spring break. While we were gone, our dog somehow got into a childproof case of Tylenol, and my neighbor's son took our dog to the veterinary hospital and then nursed her back to health until we could get home. (She's totally fine now.)

We've played innocent pranks with the family two houses down, and one time, while they were on a little weekend getaway, we noticed that their gas meter out back had been busted. So we called the fire department and made sure everything got fixed and was safe for them when they returned.

And then there's one neighbor whose dog, Bates, is . . . well, he's precious and he's hilarious, but he's wild and he loves to run. He gets out at least one morning every week, and we'll have half the street outside trying to catch him. They all know our cat Wednesday. Wednesday has even worked her way into a few of their houses via doggie doors and has scared the living daylights out of them.

(That's right. I am now a cat owner and I officially owe you an apology for saying cats were disgusting in *I'll Be There (But I'll Be Wearing Sweatpants)*. I start off every day holding her like a newborn baby and petting her like she is the greatest thing that's ever happened to planet Earth. Sometimes I sing to her, and I most certainly do own a tea towel that says "Cat Mom." I've become one of those people.)

The point is that there are good, good people who live twenty yards away from you that you may not even know. How sad. My grandma knew every single one of her neighbors. In fact, when she suffered her brain aneurysm years ago, it was a neighbor who saved her life and took her to the hospital. But for whatever reason, relationships with the people who live closest to us don't feel as easy anymore. We are super connected to people on our Facebook pages. We keep up with people who are near strangers who we haven't had a single interaction with since college. But when it comes to people two doors down, we refuse to make any efforts, so I've compiled a list with a few easy steps you can take to build community with your neighbors.

Buy some chairs and sit outside regularly. Yes, it kind of has to be the front yard where you can interact with them and they can interact with you. No, the chairs do not need to be expensive or fancy. They just need the four legs and that's pretty much it. Friendliness tends to lead to friendships.

Encourage your kids to do a lemonade stand. It was within the first two months of us moving in, and I'd had it with my offspring begging me for money. Finally, I'd tired of the whining and told them they weren't allowed to so much as ask me for one more thing. If they wanted to earn money, it was up to them, but they were going to have to work for it.

So they decided to have a lemonade stand. They got the supplies, made the lemonade, set up shop, and the neighbors came one by one—I'm sure partly because they were curious about the new family that had moved in and partly because most people are good and most people are willing to stop and help kids. That day, I think we met at least six new neighbors. It was easy. It was natural. It was good. Not the lemonade. The lemonade was watery and germy because kids are disgusting, but getting to know the people who live in the houses around ours—that was beautiful.

Walk your dog or go for a jog at the same time every day. Routines matter. If you run into the same people for two weeks solid, conversation is likely to come about as a result. People might feel weird stopping and talking to you, but they won't hesitate to reach down and pet your dog. Dogs and kids . . . they're natural icebreakers. Use it to your advantage. And as a bonus, maybe you start walking regularly with other people in your neighborhood and maybe a friendship grows from there.

Drop off little gifts, especially around the holidays. This is my favorite one! It is so fun and it makes me so happy! I didn't do this at my old house. I honestly didn't know my neighbors because I wasn't confident enough to put in the work. I see it all differently since Jennifer. I want to be giving to the people around me. I want to know them. I know that a relationship with them—whether it be surface level or something deeper—is beneficial.

So for Halloween everybody with kids gets a little "boo bucket." At Christmas everybody gets a little Christmas basket with hot chocolate supplies (cups, cocoa packets, marshmallows, sprinkles, and Hershey's kisses). When it's Valentine's Day, I order red-heart yard signs off Amazon and we put them somewhere in everyone's front yard. During Thanksgiving we deliver little notes that say, "We're so thankful you're our neighbor!" We haven't done anything for Easter or Fourth of July, but maybe we should add that this year. I guess we'll see.

Include your neighbors when you have parties or people over. I have learned that there is a difference between entertaining and welcoming someone into your home. Entertaining feels like a lot. A lot of expectations. A lot of pressure. A lot of money. A lot of time. A lot of planning. When I entertain, I feel like I need to impress. Welcoming someone into my home, on the other hand, feels simple. Simple food. Simple dishes. Simple premise. Simple setup. When I welcome someone into my home, it has nothing to do with impressing them and everything to do with making them feel wanted. I can handle entertaining on rare occasions. However, I can handle welcoming people into my home on a regular basis.

I don't do a lot of cleaning, prepping, or fretting. I invite them into my home exactly as it is and I pray that in doing so, I make them feel safe enough to come inside exactly as they are. I genuinely believe our world needs more of this. I've learned that I will probably never have the biggest house. I will definitely never have the cleanest house. I will probably never have the most expensive furniture or the most on-trend decor. I can't win a race against the Joneses, and frankly, I'd rather not. Keep-up is a stupid game that gives out stupid prizes. I can, however, have a home that is warm, accepting, and full of joy, love, and hospitality. I want to welcome people from all different areas of my life into my home, and that includes neighbors.

Be good to the neighborhood kids. If you have kids of your own, help them get to know the neighbors. Accommodate playdates and games of hide-and-go-seek. Keep snacks handy. If there's one thing I know about kids, it's that they love a good snack. Have a stack of plastic cups where they can get their own water. (Or let them drink straight out of the water hose. We did it and look at us! We turned out fine.) If you don't have kids, this is your chance to spoil someone else's children with zero ramifications. You aren't responsible for whether they turn out to be jerks.

Go over and introduce yourself (if you haven't already) when they're outside. Walking over and saying hi is incredibly awkward. Just across the board, for all of us. On the walk over, you may forget how to properly swing your arms. I think that's normal. You may talk to yourself a little. I think that's normal too, and you'll probably run through a million scenarios in your head like "But do I give them a handshake?" "Do I go in for a hug?" "What do I say besides hi?" "OH MY WORD WHAT IF I TRIP IN THE MIDDLE OF THE STREET AND THEY HAVE TO CALL AN AMBULANCE?"

It's uncomfortable to be the one to make the first move, but somebody has to do it. The older I get, the less I want to be known as the woman who sat around and waited for things to happen to her . . . the woman who waited for an invitation, the woman who waited for an introduction, the woman who waited to make a friend. I want to be a woman who just lays it all on the line and goes for it. Life's too short for anything else.

Be willing to solve and address problems calmly and kindly when they arise (and they will arise). You share a fence with these people. Your yard touches their yard. Stuff might happen. The best you can do is confront the situation. Stay reasonable. Listen to what they're trying to say without being defensive or dismissive. Do your part to make it work, but that's all you can do. Their reactions are on them, but make sure you are keeping your side of the street clean.

Show up when there is something to celebrate or something to mourn. Bring meals when someone is in the hospital or sick. Bring flowers when someone is going through a loss of some sort. Rake their leaves, pick up the mail, or take out their trash when you know things are overwhelming in their life. Bring them a box of diapers when they have a baby. Drop off a card just to lift their spirits. Tie a balloon to their front door when they get a promotion. Show up in the same way you'd show up for a good friend. Acts of kindness go so far in building and maintaining relationships, so when you can, be there for the highs and help carry them through the lows.

Be thoughtful. You live really close to these people. The trash you toss out of your car door ends up on their porch. That dog poop you forgot to pick up in their yard probably got stepped on by one of their kids and tracked through their entire house. This isn't rocket science and it isn't complicated—just be courteous. Think about how your actions will affect them and then act accordingly.

Bake them stuff. Chocolate chip cookies, homemade salsa, rice krispies treats, *queso*. These seem to be crowd favorites and they're fairly easy to deliver from house to house, but anything you like to cook will work. Again, nothing rocket science-y here. Just every once in a while, make a little something extra, throw it on a paper plate, cover it with aluminum foil, and deliver it to a neighbor's front porch. There really is something sacred about making sure the people around us have been fed and sharing bread with them.

Ask for help and offer to help when they need a hand. Do not be too proud to ask for help. Do not be too scared to admit when you need something from a neighbor. Most people want to lend a hand, and doing favors for each other, as long as they are reciprocal, forms bonds between us as humans.

So ask to borrow that flour. Ask when you need help moving that couch. Ask for assistance when fixing a leak in your bathroom. Get their recommendations on who to call when you have plumbing issues, or when your roof needs to be repaired after a hailstorm. Ask who they used to do their kitchen remodel. People typically love to give advice and share their opinions, so give them an opportunity to do it. And when you notice them trying to unload a piece of new furniture from the back of their truck, run over and assist without being asked. If you see them having to jump-start their car, ask if they need another set of hands. When they go out of town, offer to water their plants or pick up their mail. We weren't made to do it all on our own. The greatest gift God has ever given us is salvation. The second greatest gift he's ever given us is each other.

Love your neighbor. It's biblical. And no, I don't necessarily believe that God intended us to only love the people who live next to us. I don't believe that God meant for us to take it literally, but loving your neighbor is a pretty good launching pad. I do believe that we are missing out if we make it our mission to go out and make a difference in the whole world while we overlook the people who live closest to us.

The Good

Having relationships with our neighbors comes with quite a few perks:

- It keeps us in touch with what is going on in our community.
- When we have an existing relationship with them, asking them for a quick favor is easy.
- When changes need to be made in your neighborhood, it will be easier to make it happen if you can team up with those around you.
- If you have a good rapport with them, they are more likely to understand and give you grace when conflict arises.
- When you're lonely, it's nice to have someone you can call to come over for a cup of coffee or a quick drink on the patio.
- Neighbors can turn into some of the best friends.

The Bad

Overall, because of busy schedules and demanding jobs, knowing neighbors in our culture seems to take more effort and more intentionality. Sometimes people live just a few steps away and we never know what is happening in their world.

The Takeaway

As you were reading this chapter, did any neighbors come to mind? Maybe it's the woman whose name you don't know, who is always out walking her dog at the same time every morning. Maybe it's the mom who is always unloading the groceries by herself. Who can you be a friend to? How can you help? Who is approachable? Who is available? Once you have someone in mind, pick one of those easy steps I listed and do it this week. The first step is always the hardest, but you got this.

CHAPTER 20

WELL, YOU JUST HONKED AT ME, SO NOW I'M GOING TO SIT AT THIS STOPLIGHT FOR ALL ETERNITY

A Recipe for Handling Confrontation

I (Amy) hate two things: pickles and confrontation.

(Giving some of y'all a minute to gather yourself at that pickle one. I know it cuts a few of you deep.)

And that's not even true. I actually hate a lot of other things as well, like budget meetings and when people are disrespectful to any kind of service staff. Also loose padding in sports bras that always freaking comes out in the wash. I don't care what anyone says, it is never—*never*—the same bra again.

For most of my life, I simply dealt with confrontation by not dealing with confrontation. I knew my mom was mad at me? I'd hide. A friend wanted to talk? Too bad. I was busy. Yes, for twenty-four days in a row. No receptionist at the front desk and you want me to ring a bell for service? I would rather gouge my own two eyes out with a plastic fork than ding-a-ling a bell all out here in the open, *exposed*.

I can't begin to tell you the angst that any kind of confrontation, big or small, brings to my soul. You want me to tell the server that my meal came out completely wrong? Bahaha. I don't think so. I will eat later. It's fine. I'll even put some in my napkin so it looks like I ate this and no one feels awkward. Don't feel bad. My taste buds don't matter. It's my fault there's someone else's lipstick on my drinking glass. Not sure how but I promise I'm not going to inconvenience you about it. I probably should have ordered raw steak—I apologize for ordering it medium-rare. My bad. I'll cut it up and push it around for a while.

If we replaced the word "confrontation" with "understanding," maybe we'd be a little less afraid of it.

I don't want to get into an argument.

My gloves are off, and we're hanging out in a coffee shop, not a boxing ring.

I'm not looking to throw down. I'm looking to get down . . . with your feelings, so I can figure this out, and we can move forward. And this reminds me of a situation where being honest about my feelings would have helped me deepen a friendship.

One time years ago, when money was especially tight, I was hosting Thanksgiving dinner. I didn't have a lot to spend on extras, but I love hosting and I wanted something to make the evening feel special and inviting, and—honestly—something to boost my own hosting confidence. So I saved up to buy a candle from my favorite store. It smelled like actual fall. Leaves changing colors. Apples being made into cider. The weather turning colder. All of that in wax form. Something about it made me feel confident because I'm always nervous when people come over. Letting people into your kitchen, your living room, your innermost sanctuary is extreme vulnerability.

The night of the dinner I lit the candle, hit a playlist on Spotify, and started cooking. It sounds silly, but every time I looked at the wick flickering, it made me happy. Guests started to arrive and a few minutes later, I looked over at the candle and it was blown out. A friend grabbed a glass of water and said, "I hope it's okay I blew out your candle. That smell was giving me a headache." I was taken aback. Surely she wasn't talking about my candle. My beautiful, perfect fall candle.

You guys, I willed myself not to be bothered. I didn't want to be bothered; I didn't want it to be a thing. But it was most definitely a thing, and it bothered like a splinter wedged deep beyond my reach, because I never admitted why the candle was important to me. I never told her. I knew she wasn't trying to be rude. I knew that she had no idea the backstory behind the candle, and the truth was, it wouldn't have taken any kind of serious conversation. I wouldn't have wanted the candle to stay burning if it was giving one of my guests a serious headache, but I could have shared my feelings with her. I could have told her, "Hey, it's totally fine to not use that candle, but it kinda hurt my feelings that you blew it out without asking. I know you didn't know it was anything important, but things have been tight lately and I saved up for that candle in an effort to make tonight special."

I can almost guarantee she would have said, "Oh my gosh, I'm so sorry. I didn't realize it was important to you." And that would have been that. But instead, I held it in, and I let it fester. If I had had a conversation, we would have learned new things about each other that would have ultimately made us better friends. This is a trivial example, but sometimes it's those little things that are perfect practice for bigger things that might come later.

Sometimes when you're scared to have a tough conversation, you've just gotta put one foot in front of the other and start. Are you scared you won't say the right thing? Are you worried you'll freeze? Even if that happens, it's okay. Communicating is hard but it's so important, and we can't do it with closed mouths and hidden hearts. We have to step out there and risk it as gently and as humbly as we know how. It's not about having an argument; it's about gaining understanding.

And oftentimes, if we aren't abundantly cautious, closing the door on a conversation with someone can easily lead to us opening the door to a conversation with a third party so we can get things off our chest. This leads to gossip, and even worse, it leads us down a hallway of distrust. If we are going to vent about it, we need to vent about it with *them*. If we are going to let somebody in on our frustrations, we need to let it be the one we're frustrated at. Whenever possible, a situation between two people needs to stay between those two people. It gets hairy—like Bigfoot hairy— because sometimes we want someone else's opinion on how to handle things. We want to ensure that we're justified in our feelings, and we want to let some of the steam off without burning the person we are currently upset with. But we have to ask ourselves what we would prefer: things to be talked about behind our back or straight to our faces. Just because we are sitting in a house full of bitterness and unrest does not mean we need to invite others in and make it a party.

How do we have tough talks? We don't need to prepare an argument or a speech. We simply need to be ourselves, remain kind, keep the focus on connection, and be grounded in honesty. We need to ask open-ended questions with an open heart. Every single time we walk through conflict successfully, it will build us up for the next time and the time after that and the time after that.

Here are some tips I've learned along the way:

It's easier to be brave and have a conversation early than it is to bury it deep. It seems like it's easier to push the issue down and delay a confrontation, but that's just not true. When you push it down, it starts to take on a life of its own. Kind of like the hydro flask that my son forgot he left hot chocolate in for a month. None of us were prepared for the explosion that occurred in our sink last Friday night. WAS THAT A FIREWORK IN THE HOUSE? WHAT BLEW UP? WHY DOES IT SMELL LIKE VOMIT?? (Kids are gross. That's not an important part of this conversation, but I feel like it should be said.) Don't delay your confrontation so long that it explodes out of you like a big, stinky, uncontrollable mess.

It's good to let some things go. There's a major difference between letting things go and burying things deep. If your friend does something annoying or hurtful, but you know you're reading it through the lens of PMS or a bad night of sleep, it's good to learn how to shake it off and give grace. Not everything requires a confrontation. Let's have reasonable expectations of our friends. No one is going to enjoy being confronted over every little thing. In fact, habitual confrontation will quickly become unsafe territory. If your friend doesn't feel like she can ever "win" with you, she's likely to move on to a friendship where a little less tiptoeing is required. I think good questions to ask yourself are, *Was that a big deal or did it just feel like a big deal at this moment? Am I actually hurt or am I just grumpy and tired? Is this actually something that should be brought up to them or something I need to get over on my own?*

Don't be embarrassed if something got to you that doesn't seem like it "should" get to you. There's no honor in refusing to acknowledge that feelings exist. We're human, and we have human feelings—sensitive feelings, big feelings, anxious feelings, furious feelings, we have them all. It's part of the human experience, and to deny our feelings is to shut off a piece of ourselves that God intentionally placed in us.

Feelings are natural. They will happen with or without our permission. We don't have to label our feelings as positive or negative, good or bad. Feelings are feelings. They simply are. The goal is to not be completely controlled by them or use them as defense mechanisms to attack, hurt, or destroy. We acknowledge them. We name them. Sometimes we sit with them awhile and sometimes we hold hands with them, but then we go on about the business of living and giving and loving. Our feelings don't make us who we are. It's what we do with those feelings that matters most.

Share your feelings, but be slow to accuse. You don't know the whole story—that's why you're going to have a conversation. Remember, you're not confronting to place blame or to argue your point. You're confronting to understand the situation and to help your friend understand you. For example, if I had come after my friend who blew out the candle and said things like, "You were being rude and selfish to blow out my candle," that wouldn't have been helpful. That would have been awful, accusatory, and hurtful to her—and also ridiculously untrue. But I could have said, "Hey, I know it wasn't intentional, but it hurt my feelings when you flippantly blew out the candle and here's why." I might have also added that I'd been under a lot of stress lately, so I was feeling overly sensitive and I knew it. Don't be afraid to be vulnerable with your friends, especially in confrontation, but keep your fingers pointed more at the situation and less on them.

Ask questions; don't be quick to assume. You don't know what you don't know (and they don't know what they don't know either). An incredible tool is asking questions like, "Hey, when you said this, it seemed like you meant _____. Was that what you meant?"

My friend Jessica and I had an in-depth conversation one night. We didn't live in the same town, and she was explaining a situation she had recently been through. I said something along the lines of "I don't think I could sit at a table filled with drama. It would stress me out." I genuinely felt like I was being supportive of her, like I was nodding along in agreement with her frustration. However, the next day she spoke up. "Hey, I can't get this out of my head, and I feel like I need to say something. Yesterday I felt like you were accusing me of immersing myself in needless drama." She was so honest and so up front, but I was so grateful to be given the opportunity to clear the air. Hers was a friendship I valued, and if she hadn't confronted me, who knows? She may have quietly backed away from the friendship instead. Her question honestly saved the dignity of our relationship. Without meaning to, she signaled three things to me:

1. She valued me enough to fix things between us.
2. She trusted me enough to expose her feelings.
3. She was incredibly mature, confident, and honest, and hers was a friendship I would always work to keep around.

Recognize that there is legitimate risk in confrontation, but it's worth it. Was it scary? Yes. Was it hard? Yes. But we both left knowing and understanding each other better. Tough conversations are one of the ways we deepen our trust as friends. Are you safe for me to be honest about something that hurt me? If the answer is yes, you're going to get closer automatically. If you're met with a clear wall that says, "I'm not approachable, open to this, or willing to engage," that's tough, but that's also telling of the friendship.

You can't be close without being able to share the raw parts of your heart. Close friendships can't exist without honest feelings, and honest feelings typically require confrontation to work through.

You will either learn that the friendship is strong enough to withstand hard things, or you'll learn that the friendship is made of paper and was inevitably going to crumble at some point. I'm sorry it crumbled now, but maybe you're being protected from future pain.

Stay focused on being kind in any kind of confrontation.

How can I communicate my feelings without being hurtful?

Is my tone considerate or condescending?

Am I being thoughtful with my word choices?

Is there something I can do to clarify or make amends for offending them?

I ask these questions and sometimes take a step back. I am not here to let bullets fly. I'm not here to wage war. I'm here for resolution. This is my attempt at waving my white flag. I'm not perfect. I'm learning. Walking out on that stage is scary, and it's very possible I'll say the wrong line. We're only the stewards of our own hearts. I can only work to be humble and address anything I got wrong. The other stuff I have to let go.

But I also remind myself that just because someone is angry doesn't mean I necessarily did the wrong thing. (That's so, so hard for me. P.S. I think this is tough on any people pleaser.) The truth is, in friendship we should be free to gently discuss things. In friendship we should be able to communicate imperfectly (and then adjust). There should be space for confrontational, kind, and open conversation if we're going to be close. A delicate friendship will always end up sinking as soon as the waters get bumpy.

The goal of confrontation is growing closer together. You're not pushing the other person away—you're actually inviting them to know you in a more personal, more raw, more real way. You're also making attempts to see them in a more authentic light as well. You're not tearing apart, you're coming together. You're not blaming them, you're seeking clarity. Let's start viewing gentle confrontation as a tool to gain better understanding and a stronger friendship.

I am someone who always longs for peace, no matter what, no matter where, no matter when. I want peace. Confrontation doesn't always feel peaceful to me, but I have to remind myself that avoiding conflict does not equal peace. It equates to pretending very real problems don't exist when they very much do. Sometimes peace has to be made and it can't be made without addressing areas of concern with each other, which is stepping closer together. It's good to remember that.

Sometimes the right thing doesn't feel right.

Confrontation is genuinely painful for me. I'm talking stomachache. I'm talking headache. I'm talking sleepless nights. I'm talking nail beds that have been destroyed because I can't stop picking at them. Maybe even a rush or two to the bathroom, if you know what I mean. Confrontation messes with my heart, my mind, my body and, in extreme instances, my bowels.

But . . . when the situation calls for it, the situation calls for it.

Typically, when there is a situation full of confusion, questions, hurts, and messes that exists between someone I love and me, I try to ask myself whether I can get over this obstacle and move on to the next lap on my own, or whether the only way to move beyond this hurdle is to talk things through with them. Again, my first choice will always be to handle things internally, but I've ruined too many relationships by assuming I am capable of this to believe it's always the correct choice. Sometimes my way of cleaning up the mess is to avoid the awkwardness, avoid the situation, and ultimately to avoid the person. And avoidance isn't okay in a close friendship.

If you've ever been the one who was ignored, you know it is

agonizing to be left haunted with questions of, "But where did I go wrong? What happened to us? I thought things were fine."

I don't want to be the kind of friend who lives with ghosts, or the kind of friend who lives by ghosting her friends. So if I respect them, if I care about their feelings, if I value their presence, and if I want to continue doing life with them, I need to love them enough to confront them. Pushing them away silently and without an open dialogue is unfair, unjust, and unkind. They deserve to give their side of the story. They deserve my honesty, my maturity, and my willingness to lay out my problems and my pains on the table, and I deserve peace. And the only way to get peace is to tackle the hard things by approaching them with a mind empty of preconceived notions and a heart full of hope.

Confrontation won't always work out the way we want it to. It won't all go according to plan. Even when we do the right thing. Even when we say the right thing. Even when we approach it in the right manner, sometimes things still get twisted. Sometimes bringing concerns up will ultimately be the thing that lets the relationship down, but I know I appreciate when someone is friend enough to fix the things that aren't right between us. I appreciate that honesty. I appreciate that they trust me enough with these icky, sticky feelings. And so I want to be able to do the same for the people in my life.

I lived so long believing that burying any and all confrontation was the nice thing to do. It probably is, but Jesus didn't call me to be nice. He didn't call me to avoid, dodge, or put solid friendships in the grave because talking things through was burdensome and unpopular. He called me to be good. He called me to love. He called me and you to live differently and to do our friendships differently. So let's love each other enough to talk it out.

We can't expect our people to telepathically know when they've hurt, offended, angered, confused, or disappointed us.

And we can't expect them to clear the air between us if they don't even know we're having trouble breathing. If we're the one with the problem, it's on us to bring things up. It's on us to be honest with our feelings, and it's on us to seek clarification. Everything after that is on them.

All we can do is do our best, and if we're not authentic, if we keep everything walled up inside, no one will ever truly know us. So speak up, have the tough conversations, and let the people in your life who are really here *for you*, be there.

The Good

Getting better at confrontation will help us in every relationship in our lives. Yes, it's scary, but the more we do it, the better we'll get.

The Bad

Sometimes we lose people. Sometimes it goes wrong. That's a real risk. I just don't see any way to develop deep, meaningful, and long-lasting friendships without wading into these murky waters from time to time. We don't need to do it often (in fact we shouldn't); we should save it for the things that matter most. But when the situation calls for it, we do need to do it.

The Takeaway

Now that you understand the importance of confronting a friend and how to do it well, you can start taking steps to create closer friendships.

As you were going through the chapter, did a situation come to mind? Is there someone you need to have a conversation with? If so, start to think about how you would approach that conversation. If you need to, grab a paper and pen and write out everything you want to say, and then go back through the tips we gave and adjust accordingly.

It's important to point out that confrontation is tough on everyone. If it causes you to mix up your words, nervously say the wrong line, have a tough time communicating, or cry uncontrollably, it does for your friends too.

If someone has a tough conversation with you but doesn't do it perfectly, remember that it's scary business to be honest about our hurts and concerns, so approach things with a soft heart. Leave space for stumbled words and flawed communication. This is all tricky, gray-area stuff.

Be honest in your feedback, but shower them with grace. Instead of pouncing if they say something you don't like, ask for clarification. Instead of building walls when things get tense, take a deep breath. Maybe even pause for prayer.

We're all learning, but in my experience, the best kind of friends are the ones who are trying, so those are the ones I suggest holding on to. They won't always get it right, but then again, neither will you. Instead of having an attitude of "Thank you, next" when it comes to friendships, let's be women who have an attitude of "Thank you for being in my life. I hope we can work this out."

CHAPTER 21

HOW TO WALK THROUGH PAIN WITH YOUR FRIENDS (THE KIND WHERE THERE ARE NO WORDS)

A Recipe for Loving Well, Even If You Feel Unqualified

> I think one of the greatest gifts of friendship is getting to be there. Being invited into another person's hard, their real, their mess, their magic, their pain, their joy, their everything . . . it's priceless. Being there is a gift.
> —Jess Johnston

There is some pain in this world that you're never going to have answers for, that you're never going to understand, and that you're never going to be able to spin into something positive. Not a single thing will fix it. You know the kind. Maybe you've walked through it yourself. Maybe you've walked through it with a loved one. You wish there was a manual, a road map for knowing exactly what to do and what to say, but there isn't one.

There aren't words to fix wounds that have grown that deep. There is no perfect way to show up to a situation this ugly and this unfair. We can give our "expert" advice. We can share our stories (and we will), but we feel strongly that it is exponentially more powerful to hear from others who have walked a similar journey. Throughout this chapter we'll provide the wisdom of some generous women who have shared with us how to walk beside a friend going through a specific situation.

When I (Jess) was young, one of our family friends went through a horrific loss when a sibling was in an accident. Our families were very close, and we spent long hours in the hospital beside them as they endured unimaginable pain. My friend and I paced the halls together, making endless trips to peek through the windows of the gift shop at blue and pink T-shirts that celebrated birth while we encountered death face-to-face. Everything in those long halls felt cold and sterile, as heartless and punishing as reality.

We lay on padded benches, staring at the ceiling panels while the hours moved slowly by. It was midnight when her uncle came to talk to us. He asked us if we wanted to come say goodbye. I remember that moment like it was yesterday. We went into the room where my friend's sibling was surrounded by blinking machines. The lights were dim. Her mom wept. We all held hands and we whispered our goodbyes.

There are some moments in life that define you, change you, and transform you, and that was one of mine. I remember the bright lights, the cold doorknobs, the water dispenser with tiny paper cups, but most of all I remember the way it feels to be present in pain with someone you love. I remember the way it feels to belong to a moment. The way the world stops and nothing else matters. You can feel time moving, but it seems like it's moving on without you. Like your body is there but your heart and soul are stuck somewhere else. I knew that even though I felt unqualified, I was right where I was supposed to be.

One of the most important things I learned from that moment was that it's not about what you say or do—it's about being present. There are some things that will not be fixed or solved. There's no beautiful saying you can say or a casserole so delicious that it will take away the pain. Cheese is good, but it's not that good. Only God can heal some holes.

The most important thing you can do is be there. That's it. Just be there. I believe (and I could be wrong) that when we choose to be present in those moments, God uses us as a conduit of his love and presence, his nearness. Our shoulder against their shoulder becomes his shoulder against their shoulder. Our hand on their hand becomes his. We're a space-holder, a vessel of comfort, a present reminder of peace.

I've walked through many similar moments. A spouse is deeply entrenched in addiction. A parent gets a diagnosis. A life is lost. Sickness. Grief and pain. Devastating news about someone we hold dear. I know that many of you have too.

The thing is, there's not really a how-to on walking through pain. People will have different needs and different preferences, but don't underestimate the power of simply showing up. Life can be really, really cruel. Sometimes stuff is just busy, and there are way too many balls in the air for one person to juggle on their own. It's easy to forget who you are and where you're headed. Life gets us distracted and off course. So you show up for each other.

Simply showing up is the most important piece. The fact that you cared enough to be present means so much. Nobody expects you to handle these delicate situations perfectly, but we would like to help you handle them with more confidence and more wisdom, so Amy built a small community online, and together we gathered ideas for ways that you can be "here for it" for each other.

Your friend has lost someone close to her. Someone very, very close. How do you show up as she walks through deep grief?
Jill: After I lost my daughter, I needed someone to just be there for me to talk to and cry to. Unfortunately, oftentimes people don't know what to say so they think it's best not to mention the name of the person who passed away. But we want to talk about our loved ones or hear memories from others about our loved ones.
Arcelia: I wish people would understand that each loss is different and there are different ways to grieve. There are no right words, just listening and accepting our new way of life.
Meg: Don't be there only for the funeral. Be there for the long haul. Check in weeks, months, even years later. Always let them know their grief is legitimate, and never make them feel like they should be over it. Because no matter how much time has passed, some days the wounds still feel fresh. Endure it with them and know that through the devastation, there is a closeness you will find that is beautiful.

Your friend is going through a divorce.
Desiree: I wanted people to understand that I was mourning the idea of what I thought love and marriage would be. It was more complex than just getting over my ex. I didn't believe in divorce and never thought I would be in that position, so officially closing that chapter was harder than I ever imagined.
Cinda: I felt so much shame, so I think having someone acknowledge the stress and pressure that was laid on my shoulders would have been comforting. For someone to see me. For someone to say, "I'm sorry this is happening." I wish people had stopped all of

the gossip, blaming, and bad-mouthing. Sometimes as life goes on and people change, you just don't work together anymore.

Heather: I wish they would have known how isolating divorce really is. It's scary and devastating. I wish they would have known that I needed some support. They could have shown up in a meaningful way just by being there. Letting me be a third wheel from time to time, inviting me to holiday things when they knew I was alone, stuff like that.

Your friend has lost their job.

Chelle: I needed to have a pity party for a minute. Sometimes we need to wallow a bit.

Julie: I wish they would have walked through the process with me instead of bombarding me with unwanted advice. I wish they would have checked in on me to make sure I wasn't getting depressed.

Maggie: I would have loved it if a friend had asked to grab coffee one-on-one, or just messaged me to ask how I was doing. Support would have meant so much.

Your friend has a child with a disability. Maybe it's physical. Maybe it's mental.

Erica: The most beneficial things to us have been friends who came and cleaned our house when we were admitted to the hospital for an extended period of time, family who took care of my other children, and DoorDash gift cards.

Mandy: First of all, be there for the diagnosis. Call, check on them, bring food because we are going through a wide range of emotions. Second, please invite our family to things. Being included gives us a piece of normalcy, which means more than I can express. We can't go to everything. We are going to have to turn down a lot of invitations, but please keep them coming.

Special-needs parents need friends too. And lastly, ask about our kid who is different. We love to talk about them. Ask us questions and encourage your kids to ask questions as well. Please don't ignore us, get shy, or look away. We all long to be seen.
Jamie: Don't judge. Try not to make assumptions about a mother who is doing her best. Be careful with advice and opinions, because so much of it can sound like criticism. Instead, ask questions and try to understand.

Your friend is depressed or is dealing with some extreme anxiety.
Ashley: Just be there! Come over and be present. When I'm in the throes of depression, I can't force myself to make plans or to socialize. If someone would just come over and hang out, it would help tremendously. They don't have to say anything special or do anything special. I don't expect them to fix me, but their physical presence means so much. And just because I go silent sometimes, it doesn't mean that I don't care or have forgotten them.
Kodi: I need people to know that I wanted to go to their party or meet for dinner, but I just couldn't. The guilt I feel for missing is almost as debilitating as the anxiety itself. I need people to tell me it's okay and we're still friends. Patience and reassurance is key.
Dawn: I wish they would educate themselves on how debilitating it can be and how it affects us physically as well as mentally. Showing up and checking in are both important. I wish people wouldn't bash medication or make me feel like my faith isn't strong enough.

Let me (Amy) remind you that for every mountain there's a valley, and for every rose there are numerous weeds. For every rainbow there's a storm. So you show up for each other. Don't overthink it. Don't hide because you're scared to get it wrong.

Let yourself simply be a conduit, a space-holder for a power much greater than yourself. It works.

Sometimes I think we treat people who are going through trauma and heartache like they have caution tape all over them. We don't want to hurt them more. We don't want to cause more pain. So we back off. We think we'll let the experts handle it like we're pulling over for ambulances at the scene of a wreck.

But listen, you might not be an expert on grief, crisis, or whatever it is someone is going through, but you're their friend—you're an expert on them, and that matters. You might not know what a counselor does in this situation, but you know that they like cream and three sugars in their coffee, and that is enough. Be the friend. You don't need to be the expert. Their therapist can help in ways you can't, but you can help them in ways a professional isn't able to. A professional isn't going to show up on their couch and help them fold laundry or bring them their favorite dessert. A professional isn't going to sit with them in silence on a difficult night, shoulder to shoulder. A professional isn't going to text just to check in.

A more appropriate label for someone going through something hard is "be gentle and handle with care." Be soft. Be observant and respectful of what they're going through, but don't stop showing up.

If you're looking for ideas on how to be more practically helpful, I ran across this idea online and am unsure who came up with it, but it's genius. Rather than saying, "Anything you need, I'm here," try offering things that are more specific so they don't have to do the thinking.

Try writing a card like this:

Hey friend,

    I'm here. I'm so sorry you're going through this, and I want to help you in whatever ways I can. Please choose something that would be most helpful to you right now (or all five).

Household chores: laundry, cleaning, grocery shopping, whatever you need.

Take the kids all day.

Freezer meals that you can pop in the oven.

Going with you to do hard things. Something hard on your list and you want support, I'm there.

Being there. No expectation. Want me to just be around? I'm here for it.

    If none of these sound nice, that's okay, I just want you to know I love you.

One of my favorite Bible verses is Esther 4:14. I remember it when I feel scared or unqualified for the task at hand: "Who knows but that you have come to your royal position for such a time as this?" (NIV).

Friendship doesn't just connect us to each other. In some ways it connects us to our Maker. It is a gift like none other. It is a privilege. It's holding an honorary position in someone else's life. Maybe "royal" is taking it too far, but I see the similarity. I don't know what brought you to this moment. I don't know why this person is your person during this awful season. I don't know why you're standing here today. Maybe you feel unqualified, maybe you feel in over your head, but let me ask you this: What if you are here right now for such a time as this? What if you're walking alongside them for a reason, and the reason is this moment? What if God has prepared you more than you'll ever know? You just be you, and let God be him. You've got this and he's got you.

The Good

I can't stress enough what an honor it is to walk with someone through their hard. It is holy. Don't miss this moment. Stay present the best you can. Take care of yourself, too (you'll need it), but remember the honor it is to be in this moment for such a time as this. It's no accident you're here.

The Bad

I wish that we never had to go through awful things, I wish we could snap our fingers and take pain away from the people we love. We can't, and that's so hard, but we do get to walk with them arm in arm, hand in hand, and that's sacred.

The Takeaway

Make this your intention, and if you want to, screenshot it for a friend who is going through a hard time:

Dear Friend,

When you go through hard things, I want you to know I am here. I'm not an expert of much. I'm not a therapist or a psychologist (although I will listen to you until you're all out of words). I'm not a doctor or a nurse. I'm not really a professional of anything. But don't count me out, because there's one thing I am an expert on and that's an expert on you. I know the way you like your coffee, and I'll bring you one every day till this season is through. I know where your dishes go and where all your groceries go too. I know where the broom and dustpan are and where the kids' clothes go.

I know your favorite places to order takeout from and what you like to eat from there without having to ask. I know the times when your kids get out of school and their favorite place for treats and their favorite playground. I know the songs to sing them at bedtime and that on sleepovers they like a little music and light on in the room.

I know that sometimes you want to just sit on the couch together and we don't have to talk. Silences with you don't make me feel uncomfortable.

I know a lot, and what I know a lot about is you, but what qualifies me most to walk with you through the storms is that I love you. I love you with my whole heart.

Love,

_____

CONCLUSION

We Ride at Dawn, I'll Bring the Snacks

It truly has been one of the greatest honors to be there for our friends, whether a given friendship is lifelong or only for a season. We've learned that sometimes the goal of friendship isn't necessarily for it to last forever. It's to be full of love, light, laughter, and truth while it's ours. Even short seasons can produce good fruit.

We can't promise you that your friendships will always be amazing. We can't promise you won't ever be hurt or let down. What we *can* promise you is that if you choose to live generously in friendship, give of yourself, and love well without expectation of return—*that* will most definitely change your life.

So if you get kicked, if you get hurt, if you get disappointed, please remember that your love has not been lost. Even if someone didn't value it or see it, it changed *your* life, because that's the nature of giving. Sure, it can change the life of the recipient, but more than that, we know it will forever change the life of the giver.

We don't know a lot, but what we do know is that generosity, love, kindness, and giving away the gift of friendship—it's always powerful, every single time. And even if someone rejects it or is undeserving or ends up breaking our heart, our gift still matters. It's still worth it. It still changes our life, and that's the only life we have control of anyway.

Friendship is a journey that requires much from us.

Resilience. This journey is going to take brushing ourselves off after disappointments. It's never going to be about getting it perfect. Don't be hard on yourself. Friendship isn't a race or a test. You're human—both flawed and wonderful. Give yourself so much grace for the journey.

Risk. The journey of friendship and sisterhood is never going to be completely safe. We do our best, we put on our seat belts, we follow the map, but sometimes we get derailed. Sometimes we get hurt. Sometimes we get disappointed.

Choices. It's never going to be about someone else's choices. You are the driver on this trip. You get to decide where you're headed and who you want to take with you. Don't hold back, don't wait for someone else to make the first move. You're in charge.

Process. This journey is as much about the drive as it is about the destination. Sure, we want solid, close friendships, but don't forget that there is so much beauty and wonder along the way. This drive isn't just about where we're headed—it's about where we are right now, and it's also about making sure you bring really good snacks.

Courage. This journey is going to take courage and strength. It's going to require that you step out of your comfort zone and grow in areas that you feel weak in.

Grace. It's going to require grace. Ever ridden with someone for so long that they fart and it smells like that Subway sandwich they just ate, and you roll down the windows screaming because it's so bad? Stuff's gonna come up, people are going to stink sometimes, and you're going to have to show grace and hang on to it like crazy.

Awareness. This journey is going to require that you learn about yourself and become more self-aware. The way you drive too slowly when you're getting tired? Gonna need to work on that.

Vulnerability. And it will require vulnerability. No one wants to talk about nothing for a bazillion hours. You can't be known unless you let yourself be known.

Listening. This journey is going to require that you get good at listening and hearing, because it's not just about you, it's about the people you've got riding alongside you too.

You don't have to choose this journey (of course you don't). If it sounds too hard, honestly, we get it and we don't blame you. But if you feel like you just can't do it, we beg to differ. We think you can, and if you need someone to link arms with you along the way, we're right here with you—seat belts on, playlists set, and snacks on point. We don't know everything that we'll encounter. We don't know all the epic places we'll visit or the things we'll see. We don't know every conversation we'll have or every experience we'll cherish. We also don't know what kind of setbacks we'll face, like flat tires and lost keys.

But this journey is going to be worth it.

We're here for it. Are you?

NOTES

Chapter 4: I See Your Lips Moving, But I Have No Idea What You're Saying

1. Ted Lasso, "Be Curious, Not Judgmental," posted by Ted Lasso Reacts, April 24, 2021, YouTube video, 2:14, https://www.youtube.com/watch?v=i_FofLSherM.

Chapter 6: I'm Sorry, But Did You Just Say What I Think You Said?

1. Diana I. Tamir and Jason P. Mitchell, "Disclosing Information About the Self Is Intrinsically Rewarding," *Proceedings of the National Academy of Sciences* 109, no. 21 (May 2012): 8038–43, https://doi.org/10.1073/pnas.1202129109.

Chapter 7: I Would Rather Eat Soggy Cheetos Than Admit I'm Wrong

1. Rick Warren, *The Purpose-Driven Life: What on Earth Am I Here For?* (Grand Rapids: Zondervan, 2002), 148.

Chapter 8: Sometimes People Suck

1. Thaneeya McArdle, "Understanding Abstract Art," Art Is Fun, accessed July 27, 2023, https://www.art-is-fun.com/understanding-abstract-art.

Chapter 9: I'm Scared of Snakes, Porta Potties, and Being Ghosted

1. Miller McPherson, Lynn Smith-Lovin, and Matthew E. Brashears, "Social Isolation in America: Changes in Core Discussion Networks over Two Decades," *American Sociological Review* 71, no. 3 (June 2006): 353–75, https://doi.org/10.1177/000312240607100301.

Chapter 13: Well, That Went Over My Head

1. Olivia Guy Evans and Saul Mcleod, "5 Love Languages: How to Show Love & Improve Relationships," Simply Psychology, last updated July 21, 2023, https://www.simplypsychology.org/five-love-languages.html.
2. "The Power of Hugs and How They Affect Our Daily Health," SCL Health, July 2019, https://www.sclhealth.org/blog/2019/07/the-power-of-hugs-and-how-they-affect-our-daily-health/.

Chapter 14: What Is This? The Twilight Zone?

1. Dr. Becky Kennedy, "Why We Love the Way We Love: Attachment Styles with Dr. Becky Kennedy," January 17, 2023, in *We Can Do Hard Things*, produced by Glennan Doyle, podcast, transcript, https://momastery.com/blog/we-can-do-hard-things-ep-169/.

Chapter 15: You're Stuck with Me Like Popcorn Kernels in Your Teeth

1. Morgan Mandriota and Lori Lawrenz, "Here Is How to Identify Your Attachment Style," PsychCentral, October 13, 2021, https://psychcentral.com/health/4-attachment-styles-in-relationships.
2. Nathan W. Hudson, William J. Chopik, and Daniel A. Briley, "Volitional Change in Adult Attachment: Can People Who Want to Become Less Anxious and Avoidant Move Closer Towards Realizing Those Goals?," *European Journal of Personality* 34, no. 1 (January 2020): 93–114, https://doi.org/10.1002/per.2226.
3. Andrea Glik, "4 Things Everyone Gets Wrong About Attachment Styles," MindBodyGreen, August 29, 2019, https://www.mindbodygreen.com/articles/understanding-attachment-theory-and-how-styles-form-in-childhood.
4. Mandriola and Lawrenz, "Here Is How to Identify Your Attachment Style."
5. BetterHelp Editorial Team and Elizabeth Erban, "Ways to Change an Attachment Style: How to Create a Secure Attachment," BetterHelp, updated June 20, 2023, https://www.betterhelp.com/advice/attachment/ways-to-create-a-secure-attachment/.

Chapter 16: You Are Welcome in My Home, But Maybe Not in My Bathroom

1. Steve Alley, quoted on "Brené Brown and Ashley Brown Ruiz on Living BIG, Part 1 of 2," December 28, 2022, in *Unlocking Us*, produced

by Brené Brown, podcast, transcript, https://brenebrown.com /podcast/living-big-part-1-of-2/#transcript.

2. "Brené Brown and Ashley Brown Ruiz on Living BIG, Part 1 of 2," *Unlocking Us.*

3. Caitlin Stanaway, "The Stages of Grief: Accepting the Unacceptable," University of Washington, June 8, 2020, https://wellbeing.uw.edu /the-stages-of-grief-accepting-the-unacceptable/.

4. "Boundaries are a prerequisite for compassion and empathy." Quote from Brené Brown, "Atlas of the Heart," Brené Brown (website), accessed July 27, 2023, https://brenebrown.com/art/atlas-of-the-heart-boundaries -are-a-prerequisite-for-compassion-and-empathy/.

ABOUT THE AUTHORS

AMY WEATHERLY is the bestselling coauthor of *I'll Be There (But I'll Be Wearing Sweatpants)*. She encourages women all over the world with her viral online community Sister I Am With You as well as on her own social media pages. She's been named one of the top 20 mom bloggers to follow by MomCafe and appeared on *Good Morning America*, the *TODAY* show, and the *Tamron Hall Show*, but she spends the majority of her time hanging out with her husband, driving her kids everywhere, and doing absolutely nothing special. She loves Diet Dr. Pepper, Flair pens, and—recently—pickleball. She's probably going pro any day now.

JESS JOHNSTON lives with her husband, Graham, and four kids—Malachi (16), Scout (14), Oaklee (12), and Haven (10)—in southern California. She is originally from Montana and Nor Cal though, so don't worry; she knows 65 degrees isn't cold and she tries not to be too wimpy. She started her writing career in 2015 with her viral blog *Wonderoak* (now called *Jess Johnston*). Jess has been featured across national news platforms and awarded Motherly's writer of the year. She specializes in keeping it real in parenting, life, and friendship. Her jobs include writing, unpaid Uber driver, high school football super-fan, snack-maker, hair-brusher and occasional lice-remover, encourager, and sock picker-upper. She is an avid consumer of coffee and cheeseburgers (usually not together).